U.S. Department
of Transportation

**Federal Aviation
Administration**

MW00528935

FAA-S-8081-29

SPORT PILOT

Practical Test Standards

for

- # Airplane
  - # Flight Instructor

December 2004

FLIGHT STANDARDS SERVICE
Washington, DC 20591

SPORT PILOT

Practical Test Standards

2004

FLIGHT STANDARDS SERVICE
Washington, DC 20591

NOTE

Material in FAA-S-8081-29 will be effective December 1, 2004.

RECORD OF CHANGES

Change 1—6/9/2006

1. Deleted the additional category/class matrix; applicants for an additional category/class privileges must take a complete practical test.
2. Added the requirement for a heading indicating system to page 9, as appropriate, for all tasks that require demonstration of skill within a heading tolerance.
3. Added weather elements for inadvertent entry into IMC on page 1-2.
4. Deleted the ATC light signal requirements from airport operations page 1-10.
5. Deleted all references to repositionable landing gear, multiple pages.
6. Added the requirement for selecting a suitable emergency landing area to airplane ground reference maneuvers, page 1-24.
7. Added proficiency check materials to flight instructor characteristics and responsibilities page 4-15.
8. Created category specific examiner/instructor checklists for the flight instructor with a sport pilot rating pages 4-v−4-xxii to replace the flight instructor matrix.
9. Deleted the flight instructor matrixes. See above.

1. Page 1-10: Exception to Note added: "Single-seat applicants must be radio equipped."
2. Page 4-17: Instructor, II (Technical Subject Areas), Task C (Federal Aviation Regulations and Publications) References: change "Glider Flight Manual" to "Aircraft Flight Manual," and change Objective 2c "approved glider flight manuals" to "approved aircraft flight manuals."

FOREWORD

The Sport Pilot Practical Test Standards for Airplane and Flight Instructor has been published by the Federal Aviation Administration (FAA) to establish the standards for the knowledge and skills necessary for the issuance of a Sport Pilot Certificate and a Flight Instructor Certificate with a Sport Pilot rating.

FAA inspectors, designated pilot examiners, and flight instructors must conduct instruction, proficiency checks, and practical tests in compliance with these standards. Flight instructors and applicants should find these standards helpful during training and when preparing for the practical test or proficiency check.

/s/ 12-20-2004
_____

Joseph K. Tintera, Manager
Regulatory Support Division
Flight Standards Service

CONTENTS

SECTION 1—SPORT PILOT AIRPLANE

CHECKLISTS

AREAS OF OPERATION

SECTION 4—FLIGHT INSTRUCTOR

CHECKLISTS

FLIGHT INSTRUCTOR CERTIFICATE WITH SPORT PILOT PRIVILEGES

AREAS OF OPERATION

INTRODUCTION

General Information

The Flight Standards Service of the Federal Aviation Administration (FAA) has developed this practical test book as the standard that shall be used by FAA inspectors and designated pilot examiners (DPEs) when conducting sport pilot and flight instructor with a sport pilot rating practical tests or proficiency checks.

The word "examiner" is used throughout the standards to denote either the FAA inspector or an FAA designated pilot examiner who conducts an official practical test or proficiency check. When an examiner conducts a proficiency check they are acting in the capacity of an authorized instructor.

A proficiency check is an evaluation of aeronautical knowledge and flight proficiency IAW Title 14 of the Code of Federal Regulations (14 CFR) part 61, section 61.321 or 61.419. A proficiency check must be administered using the appropriate practical test standard (PTS) for the category of aircraft when a pilot or a flight instructor adds new category/class privileges. Upon successful completion of the proficiency check the authorized instructor will endorse the applicant's logbook indicating the added category/class of equipment that the applicant is authorized to operate. When an examiner conducts a proficiency check they are acting in the capacity of an authorized instructor.

DPEs must have designation authority to conduct sport pilot initial evaluations (Sport Pilot Examiner (SPE)) and flight instructors with a sport pilot rating initial evaluations (Sport Pilot Flight Instructor Examiner (SFIE)) per FAA Order 8710.7, Sport Pilot Examiner's Handbook.

Authorized instructors must use this PTS when preparing applicants for practical tests or proficiency checks and when conducting proficiency checks. Applicants should be familiar with this book and refer to these standards during their training.

Information considered directive in nature is described in this practical test book in terms, such as "shall" and "must" indicating the actions are mandatory. Guidance information is described in terms, such as "should" and "may" indicating the actions are desirable or permissive, but not mandatory.

FAA-S-8081-29

Change 1 (6/9/06)

The FAA gratefully acknowledges the valuable assistance provided by many individuals and organizations throughout the aviation community who contributed their time and talent in assisting with the development of this practical test standard.

This PTS may be purchased from the Superintendent of Documents, U.S. Government Printing Office (GPO), Washington, DC 20402-9325, or from http://bookstore.gpo.gov. This PTS is also available for download, in pdf format, from the Flight Standards Service web site at www.faa.gov.

The U.S. Department of Transportation, Federal Aviation Administration, Airman Testing Standards Branch, AFS-630, P.O. BOX 25082, Oklahoma City, OK 73125 publishes this PTS. Comments regarding this PTS should be sent, in e-mail form, to AFS630comments@faa.gov.

Practical Test Standards Concept

14 CFR part 61.311 specifies the AREAS OF OPERATION in which knowledge and skill must be demonstrated by the applicant before the issuance of a Sport Pilot Certificate or privileges. The CFRs provide the flexibility to permit the FAA to publish practical test standards containing the AREAS OF OPERATION and specific TASKs in which pilot competency shall be demonstrated. The FAA shall revise this practical test standard whenever it is determined that changes are needed in the interest of safety. **Adherence to the provisions of the regulations and the practical test standards is mandatory for practical tests and proficiency checks.**

Practical Test Book Description

This test book contains the following Sport Pilot Practical Test Standards.

Section 1—Airplane Single-Engine Land and Sea
Section 4—Flight Instructor (The flight instructor section contains a separate introduction in section 4.)

The Sport Pilot Practical Test Standards include the AREAS OF OPERATION and TASKs for the issuance of an initial Sport Pilot Certificate and for the addition of sport pilot category/class privileges. It also contains information on how to obtain an initial Flight Instructor Certificate with a sport pilot rating and for the addition of flight instructor category/class privileges.

Practical Test Standards Description

AREAS OF OPERATION are phases of the practical test or proficiency check arranged in a logical sequence within each standard. They begin with Preflight Preparation and end with Postflight Procedures. The examiner may conduct the practical test or proficiency check in any sequence that will result in a complete and efficient test. An authorized instructor may conduct a proficiency check in any sequence that will result in a complete and efficient test. However, the ground portion of the practical test or proficiency check shall be accomplished before the flight portion.

TASKs are specific knowledge areas, flight procedures, or maneuvers appropriate to an AREA OF OPERATION. The abbreviation(s) within parentheses immediately following a TASK refer to the appropriate class of aircraft. The meaning of each class abbreviation is as follows:

ASEL   Airplane Single-Engine—Land
ASES   Airplane Single-Engine—Sea

When administering a test using section 1 or 4 of this PTS, the TASKs appropriate to the class aircraft (ASEL and ASES) used for the test shall be included in the plan of action. The absence of a class indicates the TASK is for all classes.

NOTE is used to emphasize special considerations required in the AREA OF OPERATION or TASK.

REFERENCE identifies the publication(s) that describe(s) the TASK. Descriptions of TASKs are not included in these standards because this information can be found in the current issue of the listed reference. Publications other than those listed may be used for reference if their content conveys substantially the same meaning as the referenced publications.

These practical test standards are based on the following references:

14 CFR part 43	Maintenance, Preventive Maintenance, Rebuilding, and Alteration
14 CFR part 61	Certification: Pilots, Flight Instructors, and Ground Instructors
14 CFR part 67	Medical Standards Certification
14 CFR part 71	Designation of class A, B, C, D, and E airspace
14 CFR part 91	General Operating and Flight Rules
AC 00-6	Aviation Weather
AC 00-45	Aviation Weather Services
AC 60-22	Aeronautical Decision Making
AC 60-28	English Language Skill Standards

AC 61-65	Certification: Pilot and Flight Instructors and Ground Instructors
AC 61-67	Stall and Spin Awareness Training
AC 61-84	Role of Preflight Preparation
AC 61-134	General Aviation Controlled Flight Into Terrain Awareness
AC 90-23	Aircraft Wake Turbulence
AC 90-48	Pilots' Role in Collision Avoidance
AC 90-66	Recommended Standard Traffic Patterns and Practices for Aeronautical Operations At Airports Without Operating Control Towers
AC 91-13	Cold Weather Operation of Aircraft
AC 91-69	Seaplane Safety for FAR Part 91 Operations
AC 120-51	Crew Resource Management Training
FAA-H-8083-1	Aircraft Weight and Balance Handbook
FAA-H-8083-3	Airplane Flying Handbook
FAA-H-8083-9	Aviation Instructor's Handbook
FAA-H-8083-13	Glider Flying Handbook
FAA-H-8083-21	Rotorcraft Flying Handbook
FAA-H-8083-23	Seaplane, Skiplane, and Float/Ski Equipped Helicopter Flying Handbook
FAA-H-8083-25	Pilot's Handbook of Aeronautical Knowledge
AIM	Aeronautical Information Manual
AFD	Airport Facility Directory
NOTAMs	Notices to Airmen
Other	Pilot Operating Handbook/ FAA-Approved Flight Manual Aeronautical Navigation Charts Seaplane Supplement

The Objective lists the important elements that must be satisfactorily performed to demonstrate competency in a TASK. The Objective includes:

1. specifically what the applicant should be able to do;
2. conditions under which the TASK is to be performed;
3. acceptable performance standards; and
4. safety considerations, when applicable.

Abbreviations

14 CFR	Title 14 of the Code of Federal Regulations
AC	Advisory Circular
ADM	Aeronautical Decision Making
AFD	Airport Facility Directory
AFM	Airplane Flight Manual
AFSS	Automated Flight Service Station
AGL	Above Ground Level
AIM	Aeronautical Information Manual

ASEL	Airplane Single Engine Land
ASES	Airplane Single Engine Sea
ASOS	Automated Surface Observing System
ATC	Air Traffic Control
ATIS	Automatic Terminal Information Service
AWOS	Automated Weather Observing System
CFIT	Controlled Flight into Terrain
CRM	Cockpit Resource Management
CTAF	Common Traffic Advisory Frequency
FA	Area Weather Forecast
FAA	Federal Aviation Administration
GPO	Government Printing Office
IMC	Instrument Meteorological Conditions
METAR	Meteorological Aviation Report (Routine)
NOTAM	Notices to Airmen
NTSB	National Transportation Safety Board
PPC	Powered Parachute
POH	Pilot Operating Handbook
PTS	Practical Test Standard
RPM	Revolutions per Minute
SS	Single-seat
SUA	Special Use Airspace
TAF	Terminal Aviation Forecast
TFR	Temporary Flight Restrictions
VFR	Visual Flight Rules
WSC	Weight-shift Controlled

Use of the Practical Test Standards Book

The FAA requires that all sport pilot and sport pilot flight instructor practical tests and proficiency checks be conducted in accordance with the appropriate sport pilot practical test standards and the policies set forth in this INTRODUCTION. Applicants must be evaluated in **ALL** TASKs included in each AREA OF OPERATION of the appropriate practical test standard, unless otherwise noted.

An applicant, who holds at least a Sport Pilot Certificate seeking additional aircraft category/class privileges at the sport pilot level, must be evaluated in all the AREAS OF OPERATION and TASKs listed in the PTS.

In preparation for each practical test or proficiency check, the examiner or authorized instructor shall develop a written "plan of action." The "plan of action" shall include all TASKs in each AREA OF OPERATION, unless noted otherwise. If the elements in one TASK have already been evaluated in another TASK, they need not be repeated.

For example, the "plan of action" need not include evaluating the applicant on complying with markings at the end of the flight, if that element was sufficiently observed at the beginning of the flight. **Any TASK selected for evaluation during a practical test or proficiency check shall be evaluated in its entirety.** Exception: examiners evaluating single-seat applicants from the ground shall evaluate only those TASK **elements** that can be accurately assessed from the ground.

The examiner or authorized instructor is not required to follow the precise order in which the AREAS OF OPERATION and TASKs appear in this book. The examiner or authorized instructor may change the sequence or combine TASKs with similar Objectives to have an orderly and efficient flow of the practical test or proficiency check events.

The examiner's or authorized instructor's "plan of action" shall include the order and combination of TASKs to be demonstrated by the applicant in a manner that will result in an efficient and valid test.

The examiner or authorized instructor is expected to use good judgment in the performance of simulated emergency procedures. The use of the safest means for simulation is expected. Consideration must be given to local conditions, both meteorological and topographical, at the time of the test, as well as the applicant's workload, and the condition of the aircraft used during the practical test or proficiency check. **If the procedure being evaluated would jeopardize safety, it is expected that the applicant will simulate that portion of the maneuver.**

Special Emphasis Areas

Examiners and authorized instructors shall place special emphasis upon areas of aircraft operations considered critical to flight safety. Among these are:

1. positive aircraft control;
2. procedures for positive exchange of flight controls;
3. stall and spin awareness (if appropriate);
4. collision avoidance;
5. wake turbulence and low level wind shear avoidance;
6. runway incursion avoidance;
7. controlled flight into terrain (CFIT);
8. aeronautical decision making/risk management;
9. checklist usage;

10. spatial disorientation;
11. temporary flight restrictions (TFR);
12. special use airspace (SUA);
13. aviation security; and
14. other areas deemed appropriate to any phase of the practical test or proficiency check.

Although these areas may not be specifically addressed under each TASK, they are essential to flight safety and will be evaluated during the practical test or proficiency check. In all instances, the applicant's actions will be evaluated in accordance to the standards of the TASKs and the ability to use good judgment with reference to the special emphasis areas listed above.

Sport Pilot—Practical Test Prerequisites (Initial)

An applicant for a Sport Pilot Certificate is required by 14 CFR part 61 to:

1. be at least 17 years of age (or 16 if applying to operate a glider or balloon);
2. be able to read, speak, write, and understand the English language. If there is a doubt, use AC 60-28, English Language Skill Standards;
3. have passed the appropriate sport pilot knowledge test since the beginning of the 24th month before the month in which he or she takes a practical test;
4. have satisfactorily accomplished the required training and obtained the aeronautical experience prescribed;
5. possess a current and valid U.S. driver's license or a valid Airman Medical Certificate issued under 14 CFR part 67;
6. have an endorsement from an authorized instructor certifying that the applicant has received and logged training time within 60 days preceding the date of application in preparation for the practical test, and is prepared for the practical test; and
7. have an endorsement certifying that the applicant has demonstrated satisfactory knowledge of the subject areas in which the applicant was deficient on the airman knowledge test.

Sport Pilot—Practical Test Prerequisites (Registered Ultra-Light Pilots)

If you are a registered ultra-light pilot with an FAA-recognized ultra-light organization on or before September 1, 2004, and you want to apply for a Sport Pilot Certificate, then you must, not later than January 31, 2007 (14 CFR part 61, section 61.329):

1. meet the eligibility requirements in 14 CFR part 61, sections 61.305 and 61.23, but not the aeronautical knowledge requirements specified in section 61.309, the flight proficiency requirements specified in section 61.311, and the aeronautical experience requirements specified in section 61.313;
2. pass the knowledge test for a Sport Pilot Certificate specified in 14 CFR part 61, section 61.307;
3. pass the practical test for a Sport Pilot Certificate specified in 14 CFR part 61, section 61.307;
4. provide the FAA with a certified copy of your ultra-light pilot records from an FAA-recognized ultra-light organization, and those records must—

   a. document that you are a registered ultra-light pilot with that FAA-recognized ultra-light organization; and
   b. indicate that you are recognized to operate each category and class of aircraft for which you seek sport pilot privileges.

Sport Pilot—Additional Privileges

If you hold a Sport Pilot Certificate or higher and seek to operate an additional category or class of light-sport aircraft (14 CFR part 61, section 61.321), you must:

1. receive a logbook endorsement from the authorized instructor who trained you on the applicable aeronautical knowledge areas specified in 14 CFR part 61, section 61.309 and areas of operation specified in section 61.311. The endorsement certifies you have met the aeronautical knowledge and flight proficiency requirements for the additional light-sport aircraft privileges you seek;
2. successfully complete a proficiency check from an authorized instructor other than the one who trained you on the aeronautical knowledge areas and areas of operation specified in 14 CFR part 61, sections 61.309 and 61.311 for the additional light-sport aircraft privilege you seek;

3. complete an application for those privileges on a form in a manner acceptable to the FAA and present this application to the authorized instructor who conducted the proficiency check specified in above paragraph;
4. receive a logbook endorsement from the instructor who conducted the proficiency check specified in 2 above, certifying you are proficient in the applicable areas of operation and aeronautical knowledge areas and that you are authorized for the additional category and class light-sport aircraft privilege.

Aircraft and Equipment Required for the Practical Test/Proficiency Check

The applicant for a Sport Pilot Certificate is required in accordance with 14 CFR part 61, section 61.45, to provide an aircraft that has a current airworthiness certificate and is in a condition for safe flight, for use during the practical test or proficiency check. This section further requires that the aircraft must:

1. be of U.S., foreign or military registry of the same category, class, and type, if applicable, for the certificate or privileges for which the applicant is applying;
2. have fully functioning dual controls, except as provided for in 14 CFR part 61, section 61.45(c), (e), and (f); and
3. be capable of performing all AREAS OF OPERATION appropriate to the privileges sought and have no operating limitations, which prohibit its use in any of the AREAS OF OPERATION, required for the practical test or proficiency check.
4. have an altitude, airspeed, and a heading indicating system, as appropriate, for all tasks that require demonstration of skill within an altitude/airspeed/heading tolerance.

The aircraft utilized for sport pilot and sport pilot flight instructor practical tests and proficiency checks must be a light-sport aircraft as defined in 14 CFR part 1.

Single-Seat Aircraft Practical Test

Applicants for a Sport Pilot Certificate may elect to take their test in a single-seat aircraft. The FAA established in 14 CFR part 61, section 61.45(f) specific requirements to allow a practical test for a Sport Pilot Certificate only. This provision does not allow a practical test for a Flight Instructor Certificate or Recreation Pilot Certificate or higher to be conducted in a light-sport aircraft that has a single-pilot seat.

With certain limitations, the practical test for a Sport Pilot Certificate may be conducted from the ground by an examiner. The examiner must agree to conduct the practical test in a single-seat aircraft and must ensure that the practical test is conducted in accordance with the sport pilot practical test standards for single-seat aircraft. **Knowledge of all TASKs applicable to their category/class of aircraft will be evaluated orally.** Single-seat sport pilots shall demonstrate competency in those specific TASKs identified by a NOTE in the AREA OF OPERATION for a single-seat practical test and any other TASKs selected by the examiner. Examiners evaluating single-seat applicants from the ground shall evaluate only those TASK **elements** that can be accurately assessed from the ground.

The examiner **must maintain radio contact** with the applicant and be in a position to observe the operation of the aircraft while evaluating the proficiency of the applicant from the ground.

Sport pilots taking the practical test in a single-seat aircraft will have the limitation, "No passenger carriage and flight in a single-pilot seat aircraft only" placed on their pilot certificate, per 61.45(f)(3), limiting their operations to a single-seat light-sport aircraft and no passenger carriage will be authorized.

Only an examiner is authorized to remove this limitation when the sport pilot takes a complete practical test in a two-place light-sport aircraft. This practical test may be conducted in the same or additional category of aircraft.

Upon successful completion of the practical test, the limitation will be removed, and the sport pilot is authorized to act as pilot in command in all categories of light-sport aircraft that he or she has a make and model endorsement within a set of aircraft to operate. The limitation can also be removed if the sport pilot completes the certification requirements in an aircraft with a minimum of two places, for a higher certificate or rating.

Single-Seat Aircraft Proficiency Check

Sport pilot proficiency checks may be preformed in a single-seat aircraft. The FAA believes it is appropriate for an instructor to perform a proficiency check for an additional category/class privilege to a Sport Pilot Certificate or higher, in accordance with 14 CFR part 61, section 61.321, using a single-seat light-sport aircraft, providing the authorized instructor is an examiner. When an examiner conducts a proficiency check they are acting in the capacity of an authorized instructor.

The authorized instructor must agree to conduct the practical test in a single seat light-sport aircraft and must ensure that the proficiency check is conducted in accordance with the sport pilot practical test standards for single-seat aircraft. Knowledge of all TASKs applicable to the category or class of aircraft will be evaluated orally. Those pilots seeking sport pilot privileges in a single-seat light-sport aircraft shall demonstrate competency in those specific TASKs identified by a NOTE in the AREA OF OPERATION for a single-seat proficiency check and any other TASKs selected by the authorized instructor. Authorized instructors evaluating single-seat applicants from the ground shall evaluate only those TASK **elements** that can be accurately assessed from the ground.

The authorized instructor must have radio contact and be in a position to observe the operation of the light-sport aircraft and evaluate the proficiency of the applicant from the ground.

On successful completion of a proficiency check, the authorized instructor will issue an endorsement with the following limitation "No passenger carriage and flight in a single-pilot seat aircraft only (add category/class/ make and model)" limiting his or her operations to a single-seat aircraft in this category, class, make, and model. The authorized instructor must sign this endorsement with his or her flight instructor and examiner number.

This limitation can be removed by successfully completing a proficiency check, accomplishing the additional TASKs identified in the practical test standards in a two-place light-sport aircraft in that specific category and class, in accordance with 14 CFR part 61, section 61.321. This proficiency check must be conducted in the same category and class of light-sport aircraft. Upon successful completion of the proficiency check, the applicant will be given an endorsement for the aircraft privilege sought.

Those recreational pilots or higher exercising sport pilot privileges will be required to have an endorsement for only the category and/or class of light-sport aircraft they are now authorized to act as pilot in command. A sport pilot will be required to have an endorsement for the category, class, make, and model within a set of aircraft in which he or she is now authorized to act as pilot in command.

Flight Instructor Responsibility

An appropriately rated flight instructor is responsible for training the sport pilot applicant to acceptable standards in **ALL** subject matter areas, procedures, and maneuvers included in the TASKs within each AREA OF OPERATION in the appropriate sport pilot practical test standard.

Because of the impact of their teaching activities in developing safe, proficient pilots, flight instructors should exhibit a high level of knowledge, skill, and the ability to impart that knowledge and skill to students.

Throughout the applicant's training, the flight instructor is responsible for emphasizing the performance of effective visual scanning and collision avoidance procedures.

Examiner Responsibility

The examiner conducting the practical test or authorized instructor conducting the proficiency check is responsible for determining that the applicant meets the acceptable standards of knowledge and skill of each TASK within each appropriate AREA OF OPERATION. Since there is no formal division between the "oral" and "skill" portions of the practical test or proficiency check, this oral portion becomes an ongoing process throughout the test. Oral questioning, to determine the applicant's knowledge of TASKs and related safety factors, should be used judiciously at all times, especially during the flight portion of the practical test or proficiency check. Examiners and authorized instructors shall test to the greatest extent practicable the applicant's correlative abilities rather than mere rote enumeration of facts throughout the practical test or proficiency check.

If the examiner or authorized instructor determines that a TASK is incomplete, or the outcome uncertain, the examiner may require the applicant to repeat that TASK, or portions of that TASK. This provision has been made in the interest of fairness and does not mean that instruction, practice, or the repeating of an unsatisfactory TASK is permitted during the certification process. When practical, the remaining TASKs of the practical test or proficiency check phase should be completed before repeating the questionable TASK.

The examiner or authorized instructor shall use scenarios when applicable to determine that the applicant can use good risk management procedures in making aeronautical decisions. Examples of TASKs where scenarios would be advantageous are weather analysis, performance planning, and runway/landing area selection.

Throughout the flight portion of the practical test or proficiency check, the examiner or authorized instructor shall evaluate the applicant's knowledge and practical incorporation of special emphasis areas.

Initial Check—Sport Pilot—Satisfactory Performance

Satisfactory performance of TASKs to meet the requirements for sport pilot certification are based on the applicant's ability to safely:

1. perform the TASKs specified in the AREAS OF OPERATION for the certificate or privileges sought within the approved standards;
2. demonstrate mastery of the aircraft with the successful outcome of each TASK performed never seriously in doubt;
3. demonstrate satisfactory proficiency and competency within the approved standards;
4. demonstrate sound judgment in aeronautical decision making/risk management; and
5. demonstrate single-pilot competence in an aircraft with a single pilot station (if applicable).

Initial Check—Sport Pilot-Unsatisfactory Performance

The tolerances represent the performance expected in good flying conditions. If, in the judgment of the examiner, the applicant does not meet the standards of performance of any TASK performed, the associated AREA OF OPERATION is failed and therefore, the practical test is failed.

The examiner or applicant may discontinue the test at any time when the failure of an AREA OF OPERATION makes the applicant ineligible for the certificate. **The test may be continued ONLY with the consent of the applicant.**

If the test is discontinued, the applicant is entitled credit for only those AREAS OF OPERATION and their associated TASKs satisfactorily performed. However, during the retest, and at the discretion of the examiner, any TASK may be re-evaluated, including those previously passed.

The following are typical areas of unsatisfactory performance and grounds for disqualification.

1. Any action or lack of action by the applicant that requires corrective intervention by the examiner to maintain safe flight.
2. Failure to use proper and effective visual scanning techniques to clear the area before and while performing maneuvers.

3. Consistently exceeding tolerances stated in the Objectives.
4. Failure to take prompt corrective action when tolerances are exceeded.

When a Notice of Disapproval is issued, the examiner shall record the applicant's unsatisfactory performance in terms of the AREA OF OPERATION and specific TASK(s) not meeting the standard appropriate to the practical test conducted. The AREA(s) OF OPERATION/ TASK(s) not tested and the number of practical test failures shall also be recorded. If the applicant fails the practical test because of a special emphasis area, the Notice of Disapproval shall indicate the associated TASK. For example, SECTION 1, VIII. AREA OF OPERATION: SLOW FLIGHT AND STALLS (ASEL and ASES), TASK A: MANEUVERING DURING SLOW FLIGHT, failure to use proper collision avoidance procedures.

Proficiency Check—Sport Pilot—Satisfactory Performance When Adding an Additional Category/Class

Satisfactory performance of TASKs to add category/class privileges is based on the applicant's ability to safely:

1. perform the TASKs specified in the AREAS OF OPERATION for the certificate or privileges sought within the approved standards;
2. demonstrate mastery of the aircraft with the successful outcome of each TASK performed never seriously in doubt;
3. demonstrate satisfactory proficiency and competency within the approved standards;
4. demonstrate sound judgment in aeronautical decision making/risk management; and
5. demonstrate single-pilot competence.

When an applicant is adding a category/class privileges to his or her Sport Pilot Certificate, the authorized instructor, upon satisfactory completion of the proficiency check, shall endorse the applicant's logbook indicating that the applicant is qualified to operate the additional sport pilot category/class of aircraft. The authorized instructor shall forward FAA Form 8710-11 to Airman Registry within 10 days.

Proficiency Check—Sport Pilot—Unsatisfactory Performance When Adding an Additional Category/Class

When the applicant's performance does not meet the standards in the PTS, the examiner or authorized instructor conducting the proficiency check shall annotate the unsatisfactory performance on the FAA Form 8710-11 and forward it to Airman Registry within 10 days. A Notice of Disapproval will **NOT** be issued in this instance; rather, the applicant should be provided with a list of the AREAS OF OPERATION and the specific TASKs not meeting the standard, so that the applicant may receive additional training.

When the applicant receives the additional training in the AREAS OF OPERATION and the specific TASK(s) found deficient during the proficiency check, the recommending instructor shall endorse the applicant's logbook indicating that the applicant has received additional instruction and has been found competent to pass the proficiency check. The applicant shall complete a new FAA Form 8710-11, and the recommending instructor shall endorse the application. The authorized instructor, other than the one who provided the additional training, shall evaluate the applicant on all TASKS required by the PTS. When the applicant successfully accomplishes a complete proficiency check, the authorized instructor, shall forward the FAA Form 8710-11 to Airman Registry within 10 days and endorse the applicant's logbook indicating the airman's additional category/class privileges.

Single-Pilot Resource Management

Single-Pilot Resource Management refers to the effective use of ALL available resources: human resources, hardware, and information. It is similar to Crew Resource Management (CRM) procedures that are being emphasized in multi-crewmember operations except that only one crewmember (the pilot) is involved. Human resources "… includes all other groups routinely working with the pilot who are involved in decisions that are required to operate a flight safely. These groups include, but are not limited to: dispatchers, weather briefer, maintenance personnel, and air traffic controllers." Single-pilot Resource Management is not a single TASK; it is a set of skill competencies that must be evident in all TASKs in this practical test standard as applied to single-pilot operation.

Applicant's Use of Checklists

Throughout the practical test or proficiency check, the applicant is evaluated on the use of an appropriate checklist (if specified by the manufacturer.) Proper use is dependent on the specific TASK being evaluated. The situation may be such that the use of the checklist, while accomplishing elements of an Objective, would be either unsafe or impractical. In this case, a review of the checklist after the elements have been accomplished would be appropriate. Division of attention and proper visual scanning should be considered when using a checklist.

Use of Distractions During Practical Tests or Proficiency Checks

Numerous studies indicate that many accidents have occurred when the pilot has been distracted during critical phases of flight. To evaluate the applicant's ability to utilize proper control technique while dividing attention both inside and/or outside the cockpit, the examiner or authorized instructor shall cause realistic distractions during the flight portion of the practical test or proficiency check to evaluate the applicant's ability to divide attention while maintaining safe flight.

Positive Exchange of Flight Controls

During flight there must always be a clear understanding between the pilots, of who has control of the aircraft. Prior to flight, a briefing should be conducted that includes the procedure for the exchange of flight controls. A positive three-step process in the exchange of flight controls between pilots is a proven procedure and one that is strongly recommended.

When one pilot wishes to give the other pilot control of the aircraft, he or she will say, "You have the flight controls." The other pilot acknowledges immediately by saying, "I have the flight controls." The first pilot says again, "You have the flight controls." When control is returned to the first pilot, follow the same procedure. A visual check is recommended to verify that the exchange has occurred. There should never be any doubt as to who is flying the aircraft.

Letter of Discontinuance

When a practical test is discontinued for reasons other than unsatisfactory performance (i.e., equipment failure, weather, or illness) FAA Form 8710-11, and, if applicable, the Airman Knowledge Test Report, shall be returned to the applicant. The examiner at that time shall prepare, sign, and issue a Letter of Discontinuance to the applicant. The Letter of Discontinuance should identify the AREAS OF OPERATION and their associated TASKs of the practical test that were successfully completed. The applicant shall be advised that the Letter of Discontinuance shall be presented to the examiner when the practical test is resumed, and made part of the certification file.

Aeronautical Decision Making and Risk Management

The examiner or authorized instructor shall evaluate the applicant's ability throughout the practical test or proficiency check to use good aeronautical decision making procedures in order to evaluate risks. The examiner or authorized instructor shall accomplish this requirement by developing scenarios that incorporate as many TASKs as possible to evaluate the applicants risk management in making safe aeronautical decisions. For example, the examiner or authorized instructor may develop a scenario that incorporates weather decisions and performance planning.

SECTION 1

SPORT PILOT

AIRPLANE

(ASEL and ASES)

SECTION 1—CONTENTS

SPORT PILOT AIRPLANE

APPLICANT'S PRACTICAL TEST CHEC

APPOINTMENT WITH EXAMINER

EXAMINER'S NAME_____

LOCATION _____

DATE/TIME _____

ACCEPTABLE AIRCRAFT

- ☐ Aircraft Documents: Airworthiness Certificate, Registration Certificate, and Operating Limitations
- ☐ Aircraft Maintenance Records: Logbook Record of Inspections/Airworthiness Directives/Safety Directives
- ☐ Pilot's Operating Handbook or FAA-Approved Flight Manual or Manufacturer's Operating Instructions

PERSONAL EQUIPMENT

- ☐ Current Aeronautical Charts
- ☐ Flight Logs
- ☐ Current AFD and Appropriate Publications

PERSONAL RECORDS

- ☐ Identification—Photo/Signature ID
- ☐ Pilot Certificate
- ☐ Medical Certificate or Driver's License
- ☐ Completed FAA Form 8710-11, Application for an Airman Certificate and/or Rating—Sport Pilot
- ☐ Airman Knowledge Test Report
- ☐ Logbook with Instructor's Endorsement
- ☐ FAA Form 8060-5, Notice of Disapproval (if applicable)
- ☐ Examiner's Fee (if applicable)
- ☐ Letter of Discontinuance (if applicable)

EXAMINER'S PRACTICAL TEST CHECKLIST

APPLICANT'S NAME_____

LOCATION_____

DATE/TIME_____

I. PREFLIGHT PREPARATION

- ☐ A. Certificates and Documents (ASEL and ASES)
- ☐ B. Airworthiness Requirements (ASEL and ASES)
- ☐ C. Weather Information (ASEL and ASES)
- ☐ D. Cross-Country Flight Planning (ASEL and ASES)
- ☐ E. National Airspace System (ASEL and ASES)
- ☐ F. Operation of Systems (ASEL and ASES)
- ☐ G. Aeromedical Factors (ASEL and ASES)
- ☐ H. Water and Seaplane Characteristics (ASES)
- ☐ I. Seaplane Bases, Maritime Rules, and Aids to Marine Navigation (ASES)
- ☐ J. Performance and Limitations (ASEL and ASES)
- ☐ K. Principles of Flight (ASEL and ASES)

II. PREFLIGHT PROCEDURES

- ☐ A. Preflight Inspection (ASEL and ASES)
- ☐ B. Cockpit Management (ASEL and ASES)
- ☐ C. Engine Starting (ASEL and ASES)
- ☐ D. Taxiing (ASEL)
- ☐ E. Taxiing and Sailing (ASES)
- ☐ F. Before Takeoff Check (ASEL and ASES)

III. AIRPORT AND SEAPLANE BASE OPERATIONS

- ☐ A. Radio Communications (ASEL and ASES)
- ☐ B. Traffic Patterns (ASEL and ASES)
- ☐ C. Airport/Seaplane Base, Runway, and Taxiway Signs, Markings and Lighting (ASEL and ASES)

IV. TAKEOFFS, LANDINGS, AND GO-AROUNDS

☐ A. Normal and Crosswind Takeoff and Climb (ASEL and ASES)
☐ B. Normal and Crosswind Approach and Landing (ASEL and ASES)
☐ C. Soft-Field Takeoff and Climb (ASEL)
☐ D. Soft-Field Approach and Landing (ASEL)
☐ E. Short-Field (Confined Area—ASES) Takeoff and Maximum Performance Climb (ASEL and ASES)
☐ F. Short-Field (Confined Area—ASES) Approach and Landing (ASEL and ASES)
☐ G. Glassy Water Takeoff and Climb (ASES)
☐ H. Glassy Water Approach and Landing (ASES)
☐ I. Rough Water Takeoff and Climb (ASES)
☐ J. Rough Water Approach and Landing (ASES)
☐ K. Forward Slip to a Landing (ASEL and ASES)
☐ L. Go-Around/Rejected Landing (ASEL and ASES)

V. PERFORMANCE MANEUVER

☐ A. Steep Turns (ASEL and ASES)

VI. GROUND REFERENCE MANEUVERS

☐ A. Rectangular Course (ASEL and ASES)
☐ B. S-Turns (ASEL and ASES)
☐ C. Turns Around a Point (ASEL and ASES)

VII. NAVIGATION

☐ A. Pilotage and Dead Reckoning (ASEL and ASES)
☐ B. Diversion (ASEL and ASES)
☐ C. Lost Procedures (ASEL and ASES)

VIII. SLOW FLIGHT AND STALLS

☐ A. Maneuvering During Slow Flight (ASEL and ASES)
☐ B. Power-Off Stalls (ASEL and ASES)
☐ C. Power-On Stalls (ASEL and ASES)
☐ D. Spin Awareness (ASEL and ASES)

IX. EMERGENCY OPERATIONS

☐ A. Emergency Approach and Landing (Simulated) (ASEL and ASES)
☐ B. Systems and Equipment Malfunctions (ASEL and ASES)
☐ C. Emergency Equipment and Survival Gear (ASEL and ASES)

X. POSTFLIGHT PROCEDURES

☐ A. After Landing, Parking, and Securing (ASEL and ASES)
☐ B. Anchoring (ASES)
☐ C. Docking and Mooring (ASES)
☐ D. Ramping/Beaching (ASES)

I. AREA OF OPERATION: PREFLIGHT PREPARATION

A. TASK: CERTIFICATES AND DOCUMENTS (ASEL and ASES)

REFERENCES: 14 CFR parts 43, 61, 91; FAA-H-8083-3, FAA-H-8083-25; AFM/POH/FAA Operating Limitations.

Objective. To determine that the applicant exhibits knowledge of the elements related to certificates and documents by:

1. Explaining—

    a. certificate privileges, limitations, and currency experience requirements.
    b. medical eligibility.
    c. pilot logbook or flight records.

2. Locating and explaining—

    a. airworthiness and registration certificates.
    b. operating limitations, placards, instrument markings, and flight training supplement.
    c. weight and balance data and/or equipment list, as applicable.

B. TASK: AIRWORTHINESS REQUIREMENTS (ASEL and ASES)

REFERENCES: 14 CFR part 91; FAA-H-8083-25; Aircraft Operating Limitations.

Objective. To determine that the applicant exhibits knowledge of the elements related to airworthiness requirements by:

1. Explaining—

    a. required instruments and equipment for sport pilot privileges.
    b. procedures and limitations for determining if an aircraft, with inoperative instruments and/or equipment, is airworthy or in a condition for safe operation.

2. Explaining—

    a. airworthiness directives/safety directives (as applicable to the aircraft brought for flight test.)
    b. maintenance/inspection requirements and appropriate record keeping.

C. TASK: WEATHER INFORMATION (ASEL and ASES)

REFERENCES: 14 CFR part 91; AC 00-6, AC 00-45, AC 61-84, AC 61-134; FAA-H-8083-25; AIM.

Objective. To determine that the applicant:

1. Exhibits knowledge of the elements related to real time weather information appropriate to the specific category/class aircraft by consulting the weather reports, charts, and forecasts from aeronautical weather reporting sources.
2. Makes a competent "go/no-go" decision based on available weather information.
3. Describes the importance of avoiding adverse weather and inadvertent entry into instrument meteorological conditions (IMC).
4. Explains courses of action to safely exit from an inadvertent IMC encounter.

D. TASK: CROSS-COUNTRY FLIGHT PLANNING (ASEL and ASES)

REFERENCES: 14 CFR part 91; FAA-H-8083-25; AC 61-84; Navigation Charts; A/FD; AIM.

Objective. To determine that the applicant:

1. Exhibits knowledge of the elements related to cross-country flight planning appropriate to the category/class aircraft.
2. Uses appropriate and current aeronautical charts.
3. Properly identifies airspace, obstructions, and terrain features.
4. Selects easily identifiable en route checkpoints, as appropriate.
5. Selects most favorable altitudes considering weather conditions and equipment capabilities.
6. Computes headings, flight time, and fuel requirements.
7. Selects appropriate navigation system/facilities and communication frequencies, if so equipped.
8. Applies pertinent information from NOTAMs, A/FD, and other flight publications.
9. Completes a navigation log, and simulates filing a VFR flight plan.

E. TASK: NATIONAL AIRSPACE SYSTEM (ASEL and ASES)

REFERENCES: 14 CFR parts 71, 91; Navigation Charts; AIM.

Objective. To determine that the applicant exhibits knowledge of the elements related to the National Airspace System by explaining:

1. Sport pilot privileges applicable to the following classes of airspace:

   a. Class B
   b. Class C
   c. Class D
   d. Class E
   e. Class G

2. Special use and other airspace areas.
3. Temporary flight restrictions (TFRs).

F. TASK: OPERATION OF SYSTEMS (ASEL and ASES)

REFERENCES: FAA-H-8083-25; AFM/POH.

Objective. To determine that the applicant exhibits knowledge of the elements related to the operation of systems on the light-sport aircraft provided for the flight test by explaining at least three (3) of the following systems, if applicable:

1. Primary flight controls and trim
2. Flaps and lift-enhancing devices
3. Water rudders
4. Powerplant and propeller
5. Landing gear, brakes, and steering
6. Fuel, oil, and hydraulic
7. Electrical
8. Avionics
9. Pitot-static, vacuum/pressure, and associated flight instruments

G. TASK: AEROMEDICAL FACTORS (ASEL and ASES)

REFERENCES: FAA-H-8083-25; AIM.

Objective.   To determine that the applicant exhibits knowledge of the elements related to aeromedical factors by explaining:

1. The effects of alcohol, drugs, and over-the-counter medications.
2. The symptoms, causes, effects, and corrective actions of at least three (3) of the following—

   a. hypoxia
   b. hyperventilation
   c. middle ear and sinus problems
   d. spatial disorientation
   e. motion sickness
   f. carbon monoxide poisoning
   g. stress and fatigue
   h. dehydration
   i. hypothermia

H. TASK: WATER AND SEAPLANE CHARACTERISTICS (ASES)

REFERENCE: FAA-H-8083-23.

Objective.   To determine that the applicant exhibits knowledge of the elements related to water and seaplane characteristics by explaining:

1. The characteristics of a water surface as affected by features, such as—

   a. size and location.
   b. protected and unprotected areas.
   c. surface wind.
   d. direction and strength of water current.
   e. floating and partially submerged debris.
   f. sandbars, islands, and shoals.
   g. vessel traffic and wakes.
   h. other features peculiar to the area.

2. Float and hull construction, and their effect on seaplane performance, as applicable.
3. Causes of porpoising and skipping, and the pilot action required to prevent or correct these occurrences.

I. TASK: SEAPLANE BASES, MARITIME RULES, AND AIDS TO MARINE NAVIGATION (ASES)

REFERENCES: FAA-H-8083-23; AIM.

Objective.   To determine that the applicant exhibits knowledge of the elements related to seaplane bases, maritime rules, and aids to marine navigation by explaining:

1. How to locate and identify seaplane bases on charts or in directories.
2. Operating restrictions at seaplane bases, if applicable.
3. Right-of-way, steering, and sailing rules pertinent to seaplane operation.
4. Marine navigation aids, such as buoys, beacons, lights, and sound signals.

J. TASK: PERFORMANCE AND LIMITATIONS (ASEL and ASES)

REFERENCES: FAA-H-8083-1, FAA-H-8083-23, FAA-H-8083-25; AC 61-84; AFM/POH.

Objective.   To determine the applicant:

1. Exhibits knowledge of the elements related to performance and limitations by explaining the use of charts, tables, and data if appropriate, to determine performance and the adverse effects of exceeding limitations.
2. Exhibits knowledge of the principles of weight and balance by explaining weight and balance terms and the effect of weight and balance on airplane performance.
3. Determines if weight and center of gravity will remain within limits during all phases of flight.
4. Describes the effects of atmospheric conditions on the airplane's performance.
5. Determines whether the computed performance is within the airplane's capabilities and operating limitations.

K. TASK: PRINCIPLES OF FLIGHT (ASEL and ASES)

REFERENCES: FAA-H-8083-25; AFM/POH.

Objective. To determine the applicant exhibits knowledge of basic aerodynamics and principles of flight including:

1. Forces acting on an airplane in various flight maneuvers.
2. Airplane stability and controllability.
3. Torque effect.
4. Wingtip vortices and precautions to be taken.
5. Loads and load factors.
6. Angle of attack, stalls and stall recovery, including flight situations in which unintentional stalls may occur.
7. Effects and use of primary and secondary flight controls including the purpose of each control and proper technique for use.

II. AREA OF OPERATION: PREFLIGHT PROCEDURES

NOTE: For single-seat applicants, the examiner shall select at least TASKs A, C, and D.

A. TASK: PREFLIGHT INSPECTION (ASEL and ASES)

REFERENCES: FAA-H-8083-3, FAA-H-8083-23; AFM/POH.

Objective.   To determine that the applicant:

1. Exhibits knowledge of the elements related to preflight inspection. This shall include which items must be inspected, the reasons for checking each item, and how to detect possible defects.
2. Inspects the airplane with reference to an appropriate checklist.
3. Verifies the airplane is in condition for safe flight.

B. TASK: COCKPIT MANAGEMENT (ASEL and ASES)

REFERENCES: FAA-H-8083-3; AFM/POH.

Objective.   To determine that the applicant:

1. Exhibits knowledge of the elements related to efficient cockpit management procedures, and related safety factors.
2. Organizes and arranges material and equipment in a manner that makes the items readily available.
3. Briefs occupant on the use of safety belts, shoulder harnesses, and any other required safety equipment, doors, and emergency procedures.

C. TASK: ENGINE STARTING (ASEL and ASES)

REFERENCES: FAA-H-8083-3, FAA-H-8083-23, FAA-H-8083-25; AC 91-13; AFM/POH.

Objective. To determine that the applicant:

1. Exhibits knowledge of the elements related to recommended engine starting procedures. This shall include pull starting, hand propping safety, and starting under various atmospheric conditions, if applicable.
2. Demonstrates awareness of other persons and property during start.
3. Positions the airplane properly considering structures, surface conditions, other aircraft, and the safety of nearby persons and property.
4. Accomplishes the correct starting procedure.
5. Completes the appropriate checklist.

D. TASK: TAXIING (ASEL)

REFERENCES: FAA-H-8083-3; AFM/POH.

Objective. To determine that the applicant:

1. Exhibits knowledge of the elements related to safe taxi procedures.
2. Performs a brake check if applicable, immediately after the airplane begins moving.
3. Positions the flight controls properly for the existing wind conditions.
4. Safely controls airplane direction and speed.
5. Complies with airport markings, signals, clearances, and instructions.
6. Taxis so as to avoid other aircraft and hazards.

E. TASK: TAXIING AND SAILING (ASES)

REFERENCES: FAA-H-8083-3, FAA-H-8083-23; USCG Navigation Rules;
International-Inland; AFM/POH.

Objective.   To determine that the applicant:

1. Exhibits knowledge of the elements related to water taxiing and sailing
   procedures.
2. Positions the flight controls properly for the existing wind conditions.
3. Plans and follows the most favorable course while taxiing or sailing,
   considering wind, water current, water conditions, and maritime
   regulations.
4. Uses the appropriate idle, plow, or step taxi technique.
5. Uses flight controls, flaps, doors, water rudder, and power correctly
   so as to follow the desired course while sailing.
6. Prevents and corrects for porpoising and skipping.
7. Avoids other aircraft, vessels, and hazards.
8. Complies with seaplane base signs, signals, and clearances.

F. TASK: BEFORE TAKEOFF CHECK (ASEL and ASES)

REFERENCES: FAA-H-8083-3, FAA-H-8083-23; AFM/POH.

Objective.   To determine that the applicant:

1. Exhibits knowledge of the elements related to the before takeoff
   check, including the reasons for checking each item and how to detect
   malfunctions.
2. Positions the airplane properly considering other aircraft/ vessels,
   wind, and surface conditions.
3. Divides attention inside and outside the cockpit.
4. Accomplishes the before takeoff checklist and ensures the airplane
   is in safe operating condition.
5. Reviews takeoff performance, such as airspeeds, takeoff distances,
   departure, and emergency procedures.
6. Avoids runway incursions and/or ensures no conflict with traffic prior
   to taxiing into takeoff position.
7. Completes the appropriate checklist.

III. AREA OF OPERATION: AIRPORT AND SEAPLANE BASE OPERATIONS

A. TASK: RADIO COMMUNICATIONS (ASEL and ASES)

NOTE: If the aircraft is not radio equipped, this TASK shall be tested orally for procedures ONLY. Exception: Single-seat applicants must be radio equipped.

REFERENCES: 14 CFR part 91; FAA-H-8083-25; AIM.

Objective.   To determine that the applicant:

1. Exhibits knowledge of the elements related to radio communications at airports without operating control towers.
2. Selects appropriate frequencies.
3. Transmits using recommended phraseology.
4. Acknowledges radio communications.

B. TASK: TRAFFIC PATTERNS (ASEL and ASES)

REFERENCES: FAA-H-8083-3, FAA-H-8083-25; AC 90-66; AIM.

Objective.   To determine that the applicant:

1. Exhibits knowledge of the elements related to traffic patterns and shall include procedures at airports with CTAF, prevention of runway incursions, collision avoidance, wake turbulence avoidance, and wind shear.
2. Complies with proper local traffic pattern procedures.
3. Maintains proper spacing from other aircraft.
4. Corrects for wind drift to maintain the proper ground track.
5. Maintains orientation with the runway/landing area in use.
6. Maintains traffic pattern altitude, ±100 feet, and the appropriate airspeed, ±10 knots, if applicable.

C. TASK: AIRPORT/SEAPLANE BASE, RUNWAY, AND TAXIWAY SIGNS, MARKINGS AND LIGHTING (ASEL and ASES)

REFERENCES: FAA-H-8083-23, FAA-H-8083-25; AIM.

Objective.   To determine that the applicant:

1. Exhibits knowledge of the elements related to airport/seaplane base, runway, and taxiway operations with emphasis on runway incursion avoidance.
2. Properly identifies and interprets airport/seaplane base runway, and taxiway signs, markings and lighting.

IV. AREA OF OPERATION: TAKEOFFS, LANDINGS, AND GO-AROUNDS

NOTE: For single-seat applicants, the examiner shall select all TASKS.

A. TASK: NORMAL AND CROSSWIND TAKEOFF AND CLIMB (ASEL and ASES)

NOTE: If a crosswind condition does not exist, the applicant's knowledge of crosswind elements shall be evaluated through oral testing.

REFERENCES: FAA-H-8083-3, FAA-H-8083-23; AFM/POH.

Objective. To determine that the applicant:

1. Exhibits knowledge of the elements related to a normal/crosswind takeoff and climb and rejected takeoff procedures.
2. Clears the area and positions the flight controls appropriately for the existing wind conditions.
3. Retracts the water rudders as appropriate, and establishes and maintains the most efficient planing/lift-off attitude, and corrects for porpoising and skipping. (ASES)
4. Lifts off at the recommended airspeed and/or attitude, and climbs at that airspeed/climb attitude (+10/–5 knots).
5. Retracts flaps after a positive rate of climb is established and maintains takeoff power to a safe maneuvering altitude.
6. Maintains directional control and proper wind-drift correction throughout the takeoff and climb.

B. TASK: NORMAL AND CROSSWIND APPROACH AND LANDING (ASEL and ASES)

NOTE: If a crosswind condition does not exist, the applicant's knowledge of crosswind elements shall be evaluated through oral testing.

REFERENCES: FAA-H-8083-3, FAA-H-8083-23; AFM/POH.

Objective.   To determine that the applicant:

1. Exhibits knowledge of the elements related to a normal and crosswind approach and landing.
2. Adequately surveys the intended landing area. (ASES)
3. Considers the wind conditions, landing surface, obstructions, and selects a suitable touchdown point.
4. Establishes the recommended approach and landing configuration and approach airspeed/attitude, adjusting pitch attitude and power as required.
5. Maintains a stabilized approach and recommended airspeed, or in its absence, not more than 1.3 V_{SO}, +10/–5 knots, and/or appropriate approach attitude, with wind gust factor applied.
6. Contacts the water at the proper pitch attitude. (ASES)
7. Touches down smoothly at approximate stalling speed/attitude. (ASEL)
8. Touches down at or within 400 feet beyond a specified point, with no drift, and with the airplane's longitudinal axis aligned with and over the runway center/landing path.
9. Maintains crosswind correction and directional control throughout the approach and landing sequence.

C. TASK: SOFT-FIELD TAKEOFF AND CLIMB (ASEL)

REFERENCES: FAA-H-8083-3; AFM/POH.

Objective. To determine that the applicant:

1. Exhibits knowledge of the elements related to a soft-field takeoff and climb.
2. Positions the flight controls for existing wind conditions and to maximize lift as quickly as possible.
3. Clears the area; taxis onto the takeoff surface at a speed consistent with safety without stopping while advancing the throttle smoothly to takeoff power.
4. Establishes and maintains a pitch attitude that will transfer the weight of the airplane from the wheels to the wings as rapidly as possible.
5. Lifts off at the lowest possible airspeed and remains in ground effect while accelerating to V_X or V_Y, as appropriate.
6. Establishes a pitch attitude for V_X or V_Y, as appropriate and maintains selected airspeed +10/−5 knots, during the climb.
7. Retracts flaps, if appropriate, after clear of any obstacles or as recommended by the manufacturer.
8. Maintains takeoff power to a safe maneuvering altitude.
9. Maintains directional control and proper wind-drift correction throughout the takeoff and climb.

D. TASK: SOFT-FIELD APPROACH AND LANDING (ASEL)

REFERENCES: FAA-H-8083-3; AFM/POH.

Objective. To determine that the applicant:

1. Exhibits knowledge of the elements related to a soft-field approach and landing.
2. Considers the wind conditions, landing surface, and obstructions, and selects the most suitable touchdown area.
3. Establishes the recommended approach and landing configuration, and airspeed/attitude; adjusts pitch attitude and power as required.
4. Maintains a stabilized approach and recommended airspeed, or in its absence, not more than $1.3 V_{SO}$, +10/−5 knots, and/or appropriate approach attitude.
5. Touches down softly.
6. Maintains crosswind correction and directional control throughout the approach and landing sequence.
7. Maintains proper position of the flight controls and sufficient speed to taxi on the soft surface.

E. TASK: SHORT-FIELD (CONFINED AREA—ASES) TAKEOFF AND MAXIMUM PERFORMANCE CLIMB (ASEL and ASES)

REFERENCES: FAA-H-8083-3, FAA-H-8083-23; AFM/POH.

Objective.   To determine that the applicant:

1. Exhibits knowledge of the elements related to a short-field (Confined Area-ASES) takeoff and maximum performance climb.
2. Positions the flight controls for the existing wind conditions; sets the flaps, if applicable, as recommended.
3. Clears the area; taxis into takeoff position utilizing maximum available takeoff area and aligns the airplane on the runway center/takeoff path.
4. Selects an appropriate take-off path for the existing conditions. (ASES)
5. Applies brakes (if appropriate) while advancing the throttle.
6. Establishes and maintains the most efficient planing/lift-off attitude and corrects for porpoising and skipping. (ASES)
7. Lifts off at the recommended airspeed/attitude, and accelerates to the recommended obstacle clearance airspeed/attitude or V_X
8. Establishes a pitch attitude that will maintain the recommended obstacle clearance airspeed, or V_X +10/–5 knots, until the obstacle is cleared, or until the airplane is 50 feet above the surface.
9. After clearing the obstacle, establishes the pitch attitude for V_Y accelerates to V_Y, and maintains V_Y, +10/–5 knots, during the climb.
10. Retracts the flaps after clear of any obstacles or as recommended by manufacturer.
11. Maintains takeoff power to a safe maneuvering altitude.
12. Maintains directional control and proper wind-drift correction throughout the takeoff and climb.

F. TASK: SHORT-FIELD (CONFINED AREA—ASES) APPROACH AND LANDING (ASEL and ASES)

REFERENCES: FAA-H-8083-3, FAA-H-8083-23; AFM/POH.

Objective.   To determine that the applicant:

1. Exhibits knowledge of the elements related to a short-field (Confined Area—ASES) approach and landing.
2. Adequately surveys the intended landing area. (ASES)
3. Considers the wind conditions, landing surface, obstructions, and selects the most suitable touchdown point.
4. Establishes the recommended approach and landing configuration and airspeed/attitude; adjusts pitch attitude and power as required.
5. Maintains a stabilized approach and the recommended approach airspeed/attitude, or in its absence not more than 1.3 V_{SO}, +10/−5 knots.
6. Selects the proper landing path, contacts the water at the minimum safe airspeed with the proper pitch attitude for the surface conditions. (ASES)
7. Touches down smoothly at minimum control airspeed. (ASEL)
8. Touches down at or within 200 feet beyond a specified point.
9. Maintains crosswind correction and directional control throughout the approach and landing sequence.
10. Applies brakes if equipped (ASEL), or elevator control (ASES) as necessary, to stop in the shortest distance consistent with safety.

G. TASK: GLASSY WATER TAKEOFF AND CLIMB (ASES)

NOTE: If glassy water condition does not exist, the applicant shall be evaluated by simulating the TASK.

REFERENCES: FAA-H-8083-23; AFM/POH.

Objective. To determine that the applicant:

1. Exhibits knowledge of the elements related to glassy water takeoff and climb.
2. Positions the flight controls and flaps for the existing conditions.
3. Clears the area; selects an appropriate takeoff path considering surface hazards and/or vessels and surface conditions.
4. Retracts the water rudders as appropriate; advances the throttle smoothly to takeoff power.
5. Establishes and maintains an appropriate planing attitude, directional control, and corrects for porpoising, skipping, and increases in water drag.
6. Utilizes appropriate techniques to lift seaplane from the water considering surface conditions.
7. Establishes proper attitude/airspeed and accelerates to V_Y, +10/−5 knots during the climb.
8. Retracts the flaps after a positive rate of climb is established.
9. Maintains takeoff power to a safe maneuvering altitude.
10. Maintains directional control and proper wind-drift correction throughout takeoff and climb.

H. TASK: GLASSY WATER APPROACH AND LANDING (ASES)

NOTE: If glassy water condition does not exist, the applicant shall be evaluated by simulating the TASK.

REFERENCES: FAA-H-8083-23; AFM/POH.

Objective. To determine that the applicant:

1. Exhibits knowledge of the elements related to glassy water approach and landing.
2. Adequately surveys the intended landing area.
3. Considers the wind conditions, water depth, hazards, surrounding terrain, and other watercraft.
4. Selects the most suitable approach path and touchdown area.
5. Establishes the recommended approach and landing configuration, airspeed/attitude, and adjusts pitch attitude and power as required.
6. Maintains a stabilized approach and the recommended approach airspeed, +10/−5 knots and/or attitude and maintains a touchdown pitch attitude and descent rate from the last altitude reference until touchdown.
7. Makes smooth, timely, and correct power and control adjustments to maintain proper pitch attitude and rate of descent to touchdown.
8. Contacts the water in the proper pitch attitude and slows to idle taxi speed.
9. Maintains crosswind correction and directional control throughout the approach and landing sequence.

I. TASK: ROUGH WATER TAKEOFF AND CLIMB (ASES)

NOTE: If rough water condition does not exist, the applicant shall be evaluated by simulating the TASK.

REFERENCES: FAA-H-8083-23; AFM/POH.

Objective. To determine that the applicant:

1. Exhibits knowledge of the elements related to rough water takeoff and climb.
2. Positions the flight controls and flaps for the existing conditions.
3. Clears the area; selects an appropriate takeoff path considering wind, swells, surface hazards, and/or vessels.
4. Retracts the water rudders as appropriate; advances the throttle smoothly to takeoff power.
5. Establishes and maintains an appropriate planing attitude, directional control, and corrects for porpoising, skipping, or excessive bouncing.
6. Lifts off at minimum airspeed and accelerates to V_Y, +10/−5 knots before leaving ground effect.
7. Retracts the flaps after a positive rate of climb is established.
8. Maintains takeoff power to a safe maneuvering altitude.
9. Maintains directional control and proper wind-drift correction throughout takeoff and climb.

J. TASK: ROUGH WATER APPROACH AND LANDING (ASES)

NOTE: If rough water condition does not exist, the applicant shall be evaluated by simulating the TASK.

REFERENCES: FAA-H-8083-23; AFM/POH.

Objective.   To determine that the applicant:

1. Exhibits knowledge of the elements related to rough water approach and landing.
2. Adequately surveys the intended landing area.
3. Considers the wind conditions, water, depth, hazards, surrounding terrain, and other watercraft.
4. Selects the most suitable approach path and touchdown area.
5. Establishes the recommended approach and landing configuration and airspeed/attitude, and adjusts pitch attitude and power as required.
6. Maintains a stabilized approach and the recommended approach airspeed and/or attitude, or in its absence not more than 1.3 V_{SO} +10/−5 knots with wind gust factor applied.
7. Makes smooth, timely, and correct power and control inputs during the roundout and touch down.
8. Contacts the water in the proper pitch attitude and at the proper airspeed, considering the type of rough water.
9. Maintains crosswind correction and directional control throughout the approach and landing sequence.

K. TASK: FORWARD SLIP TO A LANDING (ASEL and ASES)

NOTE: This TASK applies to airplanes capable of performing slips.

REFERENCES: FAA-H-8083-3, FAA-H-8083-23; AFM/POH.

Objective.   To determine that the applicant:

1. Exhibits knowledge of the elements related to forward slip to a landing.
2. Considers the wind conditions, landing surface, obstructions, and selects the most suitable touchdown point.
3. Establishes the slipping attitude at the point from which a landing can be made using the recommended approach and landing configuration and airspeed; adjusts pitch attitude and power as required.
4. Maintains a ground track aligned with the runway center/landing path and an airspeed/attitude, which results in minimum float during the roundout.
5. Makes smooth, timely, and correct control application during the recovery from the slip, the roundout, and the touchdown.
6. Touches down smoothly at the approximate stalling speed, at or within 400 feet beyond a specified point.
7. Maintains crosswind correction and directional control throughout the approach and landing sequence.

L. TASK: GO-AROUND/REJECTED LANDING (ASEL and ASES)

REFERENCES: FAA-H-8083-3, FAA-H-8083-23; AFM/POH.

Objective.   To determine that the applicant:

1. Exhibits knowledge of the elements related to a go-around/ rejected landing.
2. Makes a timely decision to discontinue the approach to landing.
3. Applies takeoff power immediately and transitions to climb pitch attitude for V_Y, and maintains V_Y +10/–5 knots and/or the appropriate pitch attitude.
4. Retracts the flaps as appropriate.
5. Maneuvers to the side of the runway/landing area to clear and avoid conflicting traffic, if appropriate.
6. Maintains takeoff power to a safe maneuvering altitude.
7. Maintains directional control and proper wind-drift correction throughout the climb.

V. AREA OF OPERATION: PERFORMANCE MANEUVER

A. TASK: STEEP TURNS (ASEL and ASES)

REFERENCES: FAA-H-8083-3, FAA-H-8083-23; AFM/POH.

Objective.   To determine that the applicant:

1. Exhibits knowledge of the elements related to steep turns.
2. Establishes the manufacturer's recommended airspeed or if one is not stated, a safe airspeed not to exceed V_A.
3. Rolls into a coordinated 360° turn; maintains a 45° bank.
4. Performs the task in the opposite direction, as specified by the examiner.
5. Divides attention between airplane control and orientation.
6. Maintains the entry altitude, ±100 feet, airspeed, ±10 knots, bank, ±5°; and rolls out on the entry heading, ±10°.

VI. AREA OF OPERATION: GROUND REFERENCE MANEUVERS

NOTE: The examiner shall select at least one ground reference maneuver.

NOTE: For single-seat applicants, the examiner shall select at least one ground reference maneuver.

A. TASK: RECTANGULAR COURSE (ASEL and ASES)

REFERENCE: FAA-H-8083-3.

Objective.   To determine that the applicant:

1. Exhibits knowledge of the elements related to a rectangular course.
2. Selects a suitable reference area and emergency landing area.
3. Plans the maneuver so as to not descend below a minimum altitude of 600 feet above the ground at an appropriate distance from the selected reference area, 45° to the downwind leg.
4. Applies adequate wind-drift correction during straight-and-turning flight to maintain a constant ground track around the rectangular reference area.
5. Divides attention between airplane control and the ground track while maintaining coordinated flight.
6. Maintains altitude, ±100 feet; maintains airspeed, ±10 knots.

B. TASK: S-TURNS (ASEL and ASES)

REFERENCE: FAA-H-8083-3.

Objective.   To determine that the applicant:

1. Exhibits knowledge of the elements related to S-turns.
2. Selects a suitable ground reference line and emergency landing area.
3. Plans the maneuver so as to not descend below a minimum altitude of 600 feet above the ground perpendicular to the selected reference line.
4. Applies adequate wind-drift correction to track a constant radius turn on each side of the selected reference line.
5. Reverses the direction of turn directly over the selected reference line.
6. Divides attention between airplane control, orientation and the ground track while maintaining coordinated flight.
7. Maintains altitude, ±100 feet; maintains airspeed, ±10 knots.

C. TASK: TURNS AROUND A POINT (ASEL and ASES)

REFERENCE: FAA-H-8083-3.

Objective. To determine that the applicant:

1. Exhibits knowledge of the elements related to turns around a point.
2. Selects an appropriate reference point based on wind direction and emergency landing areas.
3. Plans the maneuver so as not to descend below a minimum altitude of 600 feet above ground level at an appropriate distance from the reference point.
4. Applies adequate wind-drift correction to track a constant radius turn around the selected reference point.
5. Divides attention between airplane control and the ground track while maintaining coordinated flight.
6. Exits at the point of entry heading ±15°.
7. Maintains altitude, ±100 feet; maintains airspeed, ±10 knots.

VII. AREA OF OPERATION: NAVIGATION

A. TASK: PILOTAGE AND DEAD RECKONING (ASEL and ASES)

REFERENCE: FAA-H-8083-25.

Objective.   To determine that the applicant:

1. Exhibits knowledge of the elements related to pilotage and dead reckoning, as appropriate.
2. Follows the preplanned course by reference to landmarks.
3. Identifies landmarks by relating surface features to chart symbols.
4. Verifies the airplane's position within 3 nautical miles of the flight-planned route.
5. Determines there is sufficient fuel to complete the flight. If not, develops an alternate plan.
6. Maintains the appropriate altitude, ±200 feet and headings, ±15°.

B. TASK: DIVERSION (ASEL and ASES)

REFERENCES: FAA-H-8083-25; AIM.

Objective.   To determine that the applicant:

1. Exhibits knowledge of the elements related to diversion.
2. Selects an appropriate alternate airport, or landing area and route.
3. Determines there is sufficient fuel to fly to the alternate airport or landing area.
4. Maintains the appropriate altitude, ±200 feet and headings, ±15°.

C. TASK: LOST PROCEDURES (ASEL and ASES)

REFERENCES: FAA-H-8083-25; AIM.

Objective.   To determine that the applicant:

1. Exhibits knowledge of the elements related to lost procedures.
2. Selects an appropriate course of action.
3. Maintains an appropriate heading and climbs, if necessary.
4. Identifies prominent landmarks.
5. Uses navigation systems/facilities and or contacts an ATC facility for assistance, as appropriate.

VIII. AREA OF OPERATION: SLOW FLIGHT AND STALLS

A. TASK: MANEUVERING DURING SLOW FLIGHT (ASEL and ASES)

REFERENCES: FAA-H-8083-3; AFM/POH.

Objective. To determine that the applicant:

1. Exhibits knowledge of the elements related to maneuvering during slow flight.
2. Selects an entry altitude consistent with safety, which allows the TASK to be completed no lower than 1,000 feet AGL.
3. Establishes and maintains an airspeed at which any further increase in angle of attack, increase in load factor, or reduction in power, would result in an immediate stall.
4. Accomplishes coordinated straight-and-level flight, turns, climbs, and descents with landing gear extended and retracted as appropriate, and various flap configurations, if appropriate, specified by the examiner.
5. Divides attention between airplane control and orientation.
6. Maintains the specified altitude, ±100 feet; specified heading, ±10°; airspeed, +10/–0 knots and specified angle of bank, ±10°.

B. TASK: POWER-OFF STALLS (ASEL and ASES)

REFERENCES: AC 61-67; FAA-H-8083-3; AFM/POH.

Objective.   To determine that the applicant:

1. Exhibits knowledge of the elements related to power-off stalls.
2. Selects an entry altitude consistent with safety, which allows the TASK to be completed no lower than 1,000 feet AGL.
3. Establishes a stabilized descent in the approach or landing configuration, as specified by the examiner.
4. Transitions smoothly from the approach or landing attitude to a pitch attitude that will induce a stall.
5. Maintains a specified heading, ±10°, in straight flight; maintains a specified angle of bank not to exceed 20°, ±10°; in turning flight, while inducing the stall.
6. Recognizes and recovers promptly after the stall occurs by simultaneously reducing the angle of attack, increasing power to maximum allowable, and leveling the wings to return to a straight-and-level flight attitude with a minimum loss of altitude appropriate for the airplane.
7. Retracts the flaps to the recommended setting, after a positive rate-of-climb is establishes. (ASES)
8. Accelerates to V_X or V_Y speed and/or the appropriate pitch attitude before the final flap retraction; returns to the altitude, heading, and airspeed/appropriate pitch attitude specified by the examiner.

C. TASK: POWER-ON STALLS (ASEL and ASES)

NOTE: In some high performance airplanes, the power setting may have to be reduced below the practical test standards guideline power setting to prevent excessively high pitch attitudes (greater than 30° nose up).

REFERENCES: AC 61-67; FAA-H-8083-3; AFM/POH.

Objective. To determine that the applicant:

1. Exhibits knowledge of the elements related to power-on stalls.
2. Selects an entry altitude consistent with safety, which allows the TASK to be completed no lower than 1,000 feet AGL.
3. Establishes the takeoff or departure configuration. Sets power to no less than 65 percent available power.
4. Transitions smoothly from the takeoff or departure attitude to the pitch attitude that will induce a stall.
5. Maintains a specified heading, ±10°, in straight flight; maintains a specified angle of bank not to exceed 20°, ±10°, in turning flight, while inducing the stall.
6. Recognizes and recovers promptly after the stall occurs by simultaneously reducing the angle of attack, increasing power as appropriate, and leveling the wings to return to a straight-and-level flight attitude with a minimum loss of altitude appropriate for the airplane.
7. Retracts the flaps to the recommended setting; after a positive rate of climb is established.
8. Accelerates to V_X or V_Y speed and/or the appropriate pitch attitude before the final flap retraction; returns to the altitude, heading, and airspeed/pitch attitude specified by the examiner.

D. TASK: SPIN AWARENESS (ASEL and ASES) (Oral Only)

REFERENCES: AC 61-67; FAA-H-8083-3; AFM/POH.

Objective. To determine that the applicant exhibits knowledge of the elements related to spin awareness by explaining:

1. Aerodynamic factors that cause spins.
2. Flight situations where unintentional spins may occur.
3. Procedures for avoidance and recovery from unintentional spins.

IX. AREA OF OPERATION: EMERGENCY OPERATIONS

NOTE: For single-seat applicants, the examiner shall select TASK A.

A. TASK: EMERGENCY APPROACH AND LANDING (SIMULATED) (ASEL and ASES)

REFERENCES: FAA-H-8083-3, FAA-H-8083-23; AFM/POH.

Objective.   To determine that the applicant:

1. Exhibits knowledge of the elements related to emergency approach and landing procedures.
2. Analyzes the situation and selects an appropriate course of action.
3. Establishes and maintains the recommended best-glide airspeed ±10 knots.
4. Selects a suitable landing area.
5. Plans and follows a flight pattern to the selected landing area considering altitude, wind, terrain, and obstructions.
6. Prepares for landing or go-around, as specified by the examiner.

B. TASK: SYSTEMS AND EQUIPMENT MALFUNCTIONS (ASEL and ASES)

REFERENCES: FAA-H-8083-3; AFM/POH.

Objective. To determine that the applicant:

1. Exhibits knowledge of the elements related to system and equipment malfunctions appropriate to the airplane provided for the practical test.
2. Evaluates the situation and takes appropriate action for simulated emergencies appropriate to the airplane provided for the practical test for at least three (3) of the following—

    a. partial or complete power loss
    b. engine roughness or overheat
    c. carburetor or induction icing
    d. loss of oil pressure
    e. fuel starvation
    f. electrical malfunction
    g. vacuum/pressure and associated flight instrument malfunctions
    h. pitot/static
    i. flap malfunction
    j. inoperative trim
    k. inadvertent door or window opening
    l. smoke/fire/engine compartment fire
    m. flight control malfunction
    n. ballistic recovery system malfunction, if applicable
    o. any other emergency appropriate to the airplane

3. Follows the appropriate checklist or procedure.

C. TASK: EMERGENCY EQUIPMENT AND SURVIVAL GEAR (ASEL and ASES)

NOTE: This TASK shall be evaluated orally.

REFERENCES: FAA-H-8083-3, FAA-H-8083-23; AFM/POH.

Objective. To determine that the applicant exhibits knowledge of the elements related to emergency equipment appropriate to the following environmental conditions:

1. Mountain terrain
2. Large bodies of water
3. Desert conditions
4. Extreme temperature changes

X. AREA OF OPERATION: POSTFLIGHT PROCEDURES

NOTE: The examiner shall select Task A and for ASES applicants at least one other TASK.

NOTE: For single-seat applicants, the examiner shall select at least TASK A and all other TASKs as applicable.

A. TASK: AFTER LANDING, PARKING, AND SECURING (ASEL and ASES)

REFERENCES: FAA-H-8083-3, FAA-H-8083-23; AFM/POH.

Objective.   To determine that the applicant:

1. Exhibits knowledge of the elements related to after landing, parking, and securing procedures.
2. Maintains directional control after touchdown while decelerating to an appropriate speed.
3. Observes runway hold lines and other surface control markings.
4. Parks in an appropriate area, considering the safety of nearby persons and property.
5. Follows the appropriate procedure for engine shutdown.
6. Completes the appropriate checklist.
7. Conducts an appropriate postflight inspection and secures the aircraft.

B. TASK: ANCHORING (ASES)

REFERENCES: FAA-H-8083-23; AFM/POH.

Objective.   To determine that the applicant:

1. Exhibits knowledge of the elements related to anchoring.
2. Selects a suitable area for anchoring, considering seaplane movement, water depth, tide, wind, and weather changes.
3. Uses an adequate number of anchors and lines of sufficient strength and length to ensure the seaplane's security.

C. TASK: DOCKING AND MOORING (ASES)

REFERENCES: FAA-H-8083-23; AFM/POH.

Objective.   To determine that the applicant:

1. Exhibits knowledge of the elements related to docking and mooring.
2. Approaches the dock or mooring buoy in the proper direction considering speed, hazards, wind, and water current.
3. Ensures seaplane security.

D. TASK: RAMPING/BEACHING (ASES)

REFERENCES: FAA-H-8083-23; AFM/POH.

Objective.   To determine that the applicant:

1. Exhibits knowledge of the elements related to ramping/beaching.
2. Approaches the ramp/beach, considering persons and property in the proper attitude and direction, at a safe speed, considering water depth, tide, current, and wind.
3. Ramps/beaches and secures the seaplane in a manner that will protect it from the harmful effect of wind, waves, and changes in water level.

SECTION 4

SPORT PILOT

FLIGHT INSTRUCTOR

SECTION 4—CONTENTS

FLIGHT INSTRUCTOR

CHECKLISTS

FLIGHT INSTRUCTOR CERTIFICATE WITH SPORT PILOT PRIVILEGES

AREAS OF OPERATION

APPLICANT'S PRACTICAL TEST CHECKLIST

APPOINTMENT WITH EXAMINER:

EXAMINER'S NAME_____

LOCATION_____

DATE/TIME_____

ACCEPTABLE AIRCRAFT

- ☐ Aircraft Documents: Airworthiness Certificate
- ☐ Registration Certificate
- ☐ Aircraft Maintenance Records: Airworthiness Inspections
- ☐ Pilot's Operating Handbook or FAA-Approved Flight Manual or Manufacturer's Operating Instructions

PERSONAL EQUIPMENT

- ☐ Current Aeronautical Charts
- ☐ Computer and Plotter
- ☐ Flight Plan Form
- ☐ Flight Logs
- ☐ Current AIM
- ☐ Current Airport Facility Directory

PERSONAL RECORDS

- ☐ Identification—Photo/Signature ID
- ☐ Pilot Certificate
- ☐ Medical Certificate or Driver's License
- ☐ Completed FAA Form 8710-11, Application for an Airman Certificate and/or Rating—Sport Pilot
- ☐ Airman Knowledge Test Report
- ☐ Logbook with Instructor's Endorsement
- ☐ FAA Form 8060-5, Notice of Disapproval (if applicable)
- ☐ Examiner's Fee (if applicable)

EXAMINER'S PRACTICAL TEST CHECKLIST FOR FLIGHT INSTRUCTOR—AIRPLANE

APPLICANT'S NAME______________________________

LOCATION______________________________

DATE/TIME______________________________

I. FUNDAMENTALS OF INSTRUCTING

Note: The examiner must select TASK F and one other TASK.

- ❑ A. The Learning Process
- ❑ B. Human Behavior and Effective Communication
- ❑ C. The Teaching Process
- ❑ D. Teaching Methods
- ❑ E. Critique and Evaluation
- ❑ **F. Flight Instructor Characteristics and Responsibilities**
- ❑ G. Planning Instructional Activity

II. TECHNICAL SUBJECT AREAS

Note: The examiner must select TASK D and at least one other TASK.

- ❑ A. Aeromedical Factors
- ❑ B. Visual Scanning and Collision Avoidance
- ❑ C. Federal Aviation Regulations and Publications
- ❑ **D. Logbook Entries and Certificate Endorsements**

III. PREFLIGHT LESSON ON A MANEUVER TO BE PERFORMED IN FLIGHT

Note: The examiner must select at least one maneuver TASK.

- ❑ **A. Maneuver Lesson**

Instructor applicants must be tested in the following areas of operation appropriate to the aircraft category/class instructor privileges they seek (refer to the appropriate category/class section of the PTS). Notes listed under each area of operation identify the TASKs that must be tested. In some cases the specific TASK is identified, in other cases a minimum number of TASKs are identified.

EXAMINER'S PRACTICAL TEST CHECKLIST FOR FLIGHT INSTRUCTOR—AIRPLANE (Continued)

SEE SECTION 1 OF THE PTS

AREAS OF OPERATION

I. PREFLIGHT PREPARATION

Note: The examiner must select two TASKs.

- ☐ A. Certificates and Documents (ASEL and ASES)
- ☐ B. Airworthiness Requirements (ASEL and ASES)
- ☐ C. Weather Information (ASEL and ASES)
- ☐ D. Cross-Country Flight Planning (ASEL and ASES)
- ☐ E. National Airspace System (ASEL and ASES)
- ☐ F. Operation of Systems (ASEL and ASES)
- ☐ G. Aeromedical Factors (ASEL and ASES)
- ☐ H. Water and Seaplane Characteristics (ASES)
- ☐ I. Seaplane Bases, Maritime Rules, and Aids to Marine Navigation (ASES)
- ☐ H. Performance and Limitations (ASEL and ASES)
- ☐ J. Principles of Flight (ASEL and ASES)

II. PREFLIGHT PROCEDURES

Note: The examiner must select TASK A and one other TASK.

- ☐ **A. Preflight Inspection (ASEL and ASES)**
- ☐ B. Cockpit Management (ASEL and ASES)
- ☐ C. Engine Starting (ASEL and ASES)
- ☐ D. Taxiing (ASEL)
- ☐ E. Taxiing and Sailing (ASES)
- ☐ F. Before Takeoff Check (ASEL and ASES)

III. AIRPORT AND SEAPLANE BASE OPERATIONS

Note: The examiner must select one TASK.

- ☐ A. Radio Communications (ASEL and ASES)
- ☐ B. Traffic Patterns (ASEL and ASES)
- ☐ C. Airport/Seaplane Base, Runway, And Taxiway Signs, Markings and Lighting (ASEL and ASES)

EXAMINER'S PRACTICAL TEST CHECKLIST FOR
FLIGHT INSTRUCTOR—AIRPLANE (Continued)

IV. TAKEOFFS, LANDINGS, AND GO-AROUNDS

Note: The examiner must select one takeoff and one landing TASK in addition to TASKs K and L.

- ❏ A. Normal and Crosswind Takeoff and Climb (ASEL and ASES)
- ❏ B. Normal and Crosswind Approach and Landing (ASEL and ASES)
- ❏ C. Soft-Field Takeoff and Climb (ASEL)
- ❏ D. Soft-Field Approach and Landing (ASEL)
- ❏ E. Short-Field (Confined Area—ASES) Takeoff and Maximum Performance Climb (ASEL and ASES)
- ❏ F. Short-Field (Confined Area—ASES) Approach and Landing (ASEL and ASES)
- ❏ G. Glassy Water Takeoff and Climb (ASES)
- ❏ H. Glassy Water Approach and Landing (ASES)
- ❏ I. Rough Water Takeoff and Climb (ASES)
- ❏ J. Rough Water Approach and Landing (ASES)
- ❏ **K. Forward Slip to a Landing (ASEL and ASES)**
- ❏ **L. Go-Around/Rejected Landing (ASEL and ASES)**

V. PERFORMANCE MANEUVER

Note: The examiner must select one TASK.

- ❏ A. Steep Turns (ASEL and ASES)

VI. GROUND REFERENCE MANEUVERS

Note: The examiner must select one TASK.

- ❏ A. Rectangular Course (ASEL and ASES)
- ❏ B. S-Turns (ASEL and ASES)
- ❏ C. Turns Around a Point (ASEL and ASES)

VII. NAVIGATION

Note: The examiner must select one TASK.

- ❏ A. Pilotage and Dead Reckoning (ASEL and ASES)
- ❏ B. Diversion (ASEL and ASES)
- ❏ C. Lost Procedures (ASEL and ASES)

EXAMINER'S PRACTICAL TEST CHECKLIST FOR FLIGHT INSTRUCTOR—AIRPLANE (Continued)

VIII. SLOW FLIGHT AND STALLS

Note: The examiner must select TASKs A and D and one other TASK.

- ☐ **A. Maneuvering During Slow Flight (ASEL and ASES)**
- ☐ B. Power-Off Stalls (ASEL and ASES)
- ☐ C. Power-On Stalls (ASEL and ASES)
- ☐ **D. Spin Awareness (ASEL and ASES)**

IX. EMERGENCY OPERATIONS

Note: The examiner must select TASKs A and B.

- ☐ **A. Emergency Approach and Landing (Simulated) (ASEL and ASES)**
- ☐ **B. Systems and Equipment Malfunctions (ASEL and ASES)**
- ☐ C. Emergency Equipment and Survival Gear (ASEL and ASES)

X. POSTFLIGHT PROCEDURES

Note: The examiner must select TASK A and one other TASK for ASES.

- ☐ **A. After Landing, Parking, and Securing (ASEL and ASES)**
- ☐ B. Anchoring (ASES)
- ☐ C. Docking and Mooring (ASES)
- ☐ D. Ramping/Beaching (ASES)

INSTRUCTOR'S PROFICIENCY CHECK CHECKLIST FOR FLIGHT INSTRUCTOR—AIRPLANE

APPLICANT'S NAME_____

LOCATION_____

DATE/TIME_____

I. FUNDAMENTALS OF INSTRUCTING

Note: The instructor may select any of the below listed FOI TASKs for a proficiency check. However, these TASKs are not required on a proficiency check.

- ❑ A. The Learning Process
- ❑ B. Human Behavior and Effective Communication
- ❑ C. The Teaching Process
- ❑ D. Teaching Methods
- ❑ E. Critique and Evaluation
- ❑ F. Flight Instructor Characteristics and Responsibilities
- ❑ G. Planning Instructional Activity

II. TECHNICAL SUBJECT AREAS

Note: The instructor must select TASK D and at least one other TASK.

- ❑ A. Aeromedical Factors
- ❑ B. Visual Scanning and Collision Avoidance
- ❑ C. Federal Aviation Regulations and Publications
- ❑ **D. Logbook Entries and Certificate Endorsements**

III. PREFLIGHT LESSON ON A MANEUVER TO BE PERFORMED IN FLIGHT

Note: The instructor must select at least one maneuver TASK.

- ❑ **Maneuver Lesson**

Instructor applicants must be tested in the following areas of operation appropriate to the aircraft category/class instructor privileges they seek (refer to the appropriate category/class section of the PTS). Notes listed under each area of operation identify the TASKs that must be tested. In some cases the specific TASK is identified, in other cases a minimum number of TASKs are identified.

INSTRUCTOR'S PROFICIENCY CHECK CHECKLIST FOR FLIGHT INSTRUCTOR—AIRPLANE (Continued)

SEE SECTION 1 OF THE PTS

AREAS OF OPERATION

I. PREFLIGHT PREPARATION

Note: The instructor must select two TASKs.

- ☐ A. Certificates and Documents (ASEL and ASES)
- ☐ B. Airworthiness Requirements (ASEL and ASES)
- ☐ C. Weather Information (ASEL and ASES)
- ☐ D. Cross-Country Flight Planning (ASEL and ASES)
- ☐ E. National Airspace System (ASEL and ASES)
- ☐ F. Operation of Systems (ASEL and ASES)
- ☐ G. Aeromedical Factors (ASEL and ASES)
- ☐ H. Water and Seaplane Characteristics (ASES)
- ☐ I. Seaplane Bases, Maritime Rules, and Aids to Marine Navigation (ASES)
- ☐ H. Performance and Limitations (ASEL and ASES)
- ☐ J. Principles of Flight (ASEL and ASES)

II. PREFLIGHT PROCEDURES

Note: The instructor must select TASK A and one other TASK.

- ☐ **A. Preflight Inspection (ASEL and ASES)**
- ☐ B. Cockpit Management (ASEL and ASES)
- ☐ C. Engine Starting (ASEL and ASES)
- ☐ D. Taxiing (ASEL)
- ☐ E. Taxiing and Sailing (ASES)
- ☐ F. Before Takeoff Check (ASEL and ASES)

III. AIRPORT AND SEAPLANE BASE OPERATIONS

Note: The instructor must select TASK C.

- ☐ A. Radio Communications (ASEL and ASES)
- ☐ B. Traffic Patterns (ASEL and ASES)
- ☐ **C. Airport/Seaplane Base, Runway, And Taxiway Signs, Markings and Lighting (ASEL and ASES)**

INSTRUCTOR'S PROFICIENCY CHECK CHECKLIST FOR FLIGHT INSTRUCTOR—AIRPLANE (Continued)

IV. TAKEOFFS, LANDINGS, AND GO-AROUNDS

Note: The instructor must select one takeoff and one landing TASK in addition to TASKs K and L.

- ❑ A. Normal and Crosswind Takeoff and Climb (ASEL and ASES)
- ❑ B. Normal and Crosswind Approach and Landing (ASEL and ASES)
- ❑ C. Soft-Field Takeoff and Climb (ASEL)
- ❑ D. Soft-Field Approach and Landing (ASEL)
- ❑ E. Short-Field (Confined Area—ASES) Takeoff and Maximum Performance Climb (ASEL and ASES)
- ❑ F. Short-Field (Confined Area—ASES) Approach and Landing (ASEL and ASES)
- ❑ G. Glassy Water Takeoff and Climb (ASES)
- ❑ H. Glassy Water Approach and Landing (ASES)
- ❑ I. Rough Water Takeoff and Climb (ASES)
- ❑ J. Rough Water Approach and Landing (ASES)
- ❑ **K. Forward Slip to a Landing (ASEL and ASES)**
- ❑ **L. Go-Around/Rejected Landing (ASEL and ASES)**

V. PERFORMANCE MANEUVER

Note: The instructor must select one TASK.

- ❑ A. Steep Turns (ASEL and ASES)

VI. GROUND REFERENCE MANEUVERS

Note: The instructor must select one TASK.

- ❑ A. Rectangular Course (ASEL and ASES)
- ❑ B. S-Turns (ASEL and ASES)
- ❑ C. Turns Around a Point (ASEL and ASES)

VII. NAVIGATION

Note: The instructor must select one TASK.

- ❑ A. Pilotage and Dead Reckoning (ASEL and ASES)
- ❑ B. Diversion (ASEL and ASES)
- ❑ C. Lost Procedures (ASEL and ASES)

INSTRUCTOR'S PROFICIENCY CHECK CHECKLIST FOR FLIGHT INSTRUCTOR—AIRPLANE (Continued)

VIII. SLOW FLIGHT AND STALLS

Note: The instructor must select TASKs A and D and one other TASK.

- ❑ A. Maneuvering During Slow Flight (ASEL and ASES)
- ❑ B. Power-Off Stalls (ASEL and ASES)
- ❑ C. Power-On Stalls (ASEL and ASES)
- ❑ **D. Spin Awareness (ASEL and ASES)**

IX. EMERGENCY OPERATIONS

Note: The instructor must select TASKs A and B.

- ❑ **A. Emergency Approach and Landing (Simulated) (ASEL and ASES)**
- ❑ **B. Systems and Equipment Malfunctions (ASEL and ASES)**
- ❑ C. Emergency Equipment and Survival Gear (ASEL and ASES)

X. POSTFLIGHT PROCEDURES

Note: The instructor must select TASK A and one other TASK for ASES.

- ❑ A. **After Landing, Parking, and Securing (ASEL and ASES)**
- ❑ B. Anchoring (ASES)
- ❑ C. Docking and Mooring (ASES)
- ❑ D. Ramping/Beaching (ASES)

FLIGHT INSTRUCTOR CERTIFICATE WITH SPORT PILOT PRIVILEGES

Flight Instructor Practical Test Section Description

This section provides guidance and procedures for obtaining a Flight Instructor Certificate with a sport pilot rating and for adding privileges to an existing Flight Instructor Certificate at the sport pilot level. Information provided in the Introduction of this practical test standard also applies to this section.

The examiner or authorized instructor determines that the applicant meets the TASK Objective through the demonstration of competency in all elements of knowledge and/or skill unless otherwise noted. The Objectives of TASKs in certain AREAS OF OPERATION, such as Fundamentals of Instructing and Technical Subjects, include only knowledge elements. Objectives of TASKs in AREAS OF OPERATION that include elements of skill, as well as knowledge, also include common errors, which the applicant shall be able to describe, recognize, analyze, and correct.

The word "examiner" is used throughout the standards to denote either the FAA inspector or an FAA designated pilot examiner who conducts an official practical test or proficiency check. When an examiner conducts a proficiency check they are acting in the capacity of an authorized instructor.

At the flight instructor level, the Objective of a TASK that involves pilot skill consists of four parts. The four parts include determination that the applicant exhibits:

1. instructional knowledge of the elements of a TASK. This is accomplished through descriptions, explanations, and simulated instruction;
2. instructional knowledge of common errors related to a TASK, including their recognition, analysis, and correction;
3. the ability to perform the procedures and maneuvers included in the standards at a more precise level than that indicated in the sport pilot tolerances; and
4. the ability to analyze and correct common errors related to a TASK.

Use of the Flight Instructor Section

The FAA requires that all flight instructor practical tests and proficiency checks be conducted in accordance with the policies set forth in this practical test standard. The flight instructor applicant must be prepared to demonstrate the ability to instruct effectively in **ALL** TASKs included in the AREAS OF OPERATION appropriate to the category/class unless otherwise noted.

A proficiency check is an evaluation of aeronautical knowledge and flight proficiency IAW 14 CFR part 61, section 61.419. A proficiency check shall be administered using the appropriate PTS for the category of aircraft when a flight instructor adds new category/class privileges. Upon successful completion of the proficiency check the authorized instructor will endorse the applicant's logbook indicating the added category/class of equipment that the applicant is authorized to operate. When an examiner conducts a proficiency check they are acting in the capacity of an authorized instructor.

All of the procedures and maneuvers to be tested are included in the sport pilot practical test standards. The flight instructor section contains the AREAS OF OPERATION that are generic to all flight instructor evaluations. Flight instructors must also be tested on TASKs located in the appropriate category/class section the PTS. Those TASKs are listed in the examiner's practical test checklist and the instructor's proficiency check checklist. The mandatory TASKs are identified by a note located in each area of operation. In some cases specific TASKs are identified. In other cases the examiner/instructor selects one or more TASKs in an area of operation for evaluation. This allows for the practical test for initial certification and additional privileges to be completed within a reasonable time frame.

The term "instructional knowledge" means the instructor applicant is capable of using the appropriate reference to provide the "application or correlative level of knowledge" of a subject matter topic, procedure, or maneuver. It also means that the flight instructor applicant's discussions, explanations, and descriptions should follow the recommended teaching procedures and techniques explained in FAA-H-8083-9, Aviation Instructor's Handbook.

In preparation for the practical test or proficiency check, the examiner or authorized instructor shall develop a written "plan of action." The "plan of action" for an initial certification test shall include the required TASKs and one or more TASKs in the *Fundamentals of Instruction*, *Technical Subject Area*, and the *Preflight Lesson on a Maneuver to be Performed in Flight* AREAS OF OPERATION. Additionally, the examiner shall test the required TASK(s) listed in the examiner's practical test checklist, for the appropriate category. The "plan of action" shall always include the required TASKs noted in each AREA OF OPERATION. **Any TASK selected shall be evaluated in its entirety.**

If the applicant is unable to perform a TASK listed in the "plan of action" due to circumstances beyond his/her control, the examiner or authorized instructor may substitute another TASK from the applicable AREA OF OPERATION.

The "plan of action" used by an authorized instructor for a proficiency check administered for the addition of an aircraft category and/or class privilege to a Flight Instructor Certificate shall include TASKs required in the AREAS OF OPERATION as indicated in the instructor's proficiency check checklist in this section.

With the exception of the required TASKs, the examiner or authorized instructor shall not tell the applicant in advance which TASKs will be included in the "plan of action." The applicant shall be prepared in **ALL** knowledge and skill areas included in the standards. Throughout the flight portion of the practical test or proficiency check, the examiner or authorized instructor shall evaluate the applicant's ability to simultaneously demonstrate and explain procedures and maneuvers, and to give flight instruction to students at various stages of flight training and levels of experience.

The examiner or authorized instructor is expected to use good judgment in the performance of simulated emergency procedures. The examiner or authorized instructor shall not simulate any condition that may jeopardize safe flight or result in possible damage to the aircraft. The use of the safest means for simulation is expected. Consideration must be given to local conditions, both meteorological and topographical, at the time of the test, as well as the applicant's workload, and the condition of the aircraft used. If the procedure being evaluated would jeopardize safety, it is expected that the applicant will simulate that portion of the maneuver.

Special Emphasis Areas

Examiners or authorized instructors shall place special emphasis upon areas of aircraft operations considered critical to flight safety. Among these are:

1. positive aircraft control;
2. procedures for positive exchange of flight controls (who is flying the aircraft);
3. stall and spin awareness (if appropriate);
4. collision avoidance;
5. wake turbulence and low level windshear avoidance;
6. runway incursion avoidance;
7. controlled flight into terrain (CFIT);
8. aeronautical decision-making/risk management;
9. checklist usage;
10. spatial disorientation;
11. temporary flight restrictions (TFR);
12. special use airspace (SUA);
13. aviation security; and
14. other areas deemed appropriate to any phase of the practical test or proficiency check.

The examiner or authorized instructor shall place special emphasis on the applicant's demonstrated ability to teach precise aircraft control and sound judgment in aeronautical decision-making/risk management. Evaluation of the applicant's ability to teach judgment shall be accomplished by asking the applicant to describe the presentation of practical problems that would be used in instructing students in the exercise of sound judgment. The examiner or authorized instructor shall also emphasize the evaluation of the applicant's demonstrated ability to teach the special emphasis areas.

Although these areas may not be specifically addressed under each TASK, they are essential to flight safety and will be evaluated during the practical test. In all instances, the applicant's actions will be evaluated in accordance to the standards of the TASKs and the ability to use good judgment reference the special emphasis areas listed above.

Sport Pilot Flight Instructor Prerequisites—Initial

An applicant for a flight instructor—initial certification practical test is to:

1. be at least 18 years of age;
2. be able to read, speak, write, and understand the English language. If there is a doubt, use AC 60-28, English Language Skill Standards required by 14 CFR part 61;
3. hold at least a current and valid Sport Pilot Certificate or higher with an aircraft category and class, privilege or rating appropriate to the flight instructor rating sought;
4. have passed the fundamentals of instructing knowledge test since the beginning of the 24th month before the month in which he/she takes the practical test or meet the requirements of 14 CFR part 61;
5. have passed the appropriate sport pilot flight instructor knowledge test(s) appropriate to the category/class the applicant is since the beginning of the 24th month before the month in which he/she takes the practical test; and
6. have an endorsement from an authorized instructor certifying that the applicant has been given flight training in the AREAS OF OPERATION specified in 14 CFR part 61 and a written statement from an authorized flight instructor within the preceding 60 days, in accordance with 14 CFR part 61, that instruction was given in preparation for the practical test. The endorsement shall also state that the instructor finds the applicant prepared for the required practical test, and that the applicant has demonstrated satisfactory knowledge of the subject area(s) in which the applicant was deficient on the airman knowledge test.

Sport Pilot Flight Instructor Prerequisites—Additional Privileges

A certificated flight instructor seeking privileges to provide flight training in an additional category/class of light-sport aircraft is required by 14 CFR part 61 to:

1. hold a valid pilot certificate with ratings appropriate to the flight instructor category and class, privileges sought;
2. receive a logbook endorsement from an authorized instructor in the AREAS OF OPERATION specified in 14 CFR part 61 for the additional category/class privilege sought;
3. successfully pass a proficiency check from an authorized instructor other than the instructor who conducted the training in the AREAS OF OPERATION specified in 14 CFR part 61 for the additional category/class privilege sought; and
4. receive a logbook endorsement certifying proficiency in the required AREAS OF OPERATION and authorized for the additional category/class privilege.

Sport Pilot Flight Instructor Prerequisites—Additional Privileges— Registered Ultra-light Instructor

If you are a registered ultra-light instructor with an FAA-recognized ultra-light organization on or before September 1, 2004, and you want to apply for a flight instructor certificate with a sport pilot rating, not later than January 31, 2008 –

1. You must hold either a current and valid Sport Pilot Certificate, a current Recreational Pilot Certificate and meet the requirements of 14 CFR part 61, section 61.101(c), or at least a current and valid Private Pilot Certificate issued under this part.
2. You must meet the eligibility requirements in 14 CFR part 61, sections 61.403 and 61.23. You do not have to meet the aeronautical knowledge requirements specified in section 61.407, the flight proficiency requirements specified in section 61.409 and the aeronautical experience requirements specified in section 61.411, except you must meet the minimum total flight time requirements in the category and class of light-sport aircraft specified in section 61.411.
3. You do not have to meet the aeronautical knowledge requirement specified in 14 CFR part 61, section 61.407(a) if you have passed an FAA-recognized ultra-light organization's fundamentals of instruction knowledge test.

4. You must submit a certified copy of your ultra light pilot records from the FAA-recognized ultra-light organization. Those records must—

   a. Document that you are a registered ultra-light flight instructor with that FAA-recognized ultra-light organization; and
   b. Indicate that you are recognized to operate and provide training in the category and class of aircraft for which you seek privileges.

5. You must pass the knowledge test and practical test for a flight instructor certificate with a sport pilot rating applicable to the aircraft category and class for which you seek flight instructor privileges.

Flight Instructor Responsibility

An appropriately rated flight instructor is responsible for training the flight instructor applicant to acceptable standards in **ALL** subject matter areas, procedures, and maneuvers included in the TASKs within each AREA OF OPERATION in the appropriate category/class in this practical test standard. In addition, the rated flight instructor is required to prepare the flight instructor applicant in all TASKs in the AREAS OF OPERATION listed in section 4.

Because of the impact of their teaching activities in developing safe, proficient pilots, flight instructors should exhibit a high level of knowledge, skill, and the ability to impart that knowledge and skill to students. The flight instructor must certify that the applicant is:

1. able to make a practical application of the fundamentals of instructing;
2. competent to teach the subject matter, procedures, and maneuvers included in the standards to students with varying backgrounds and levels of experience and ability;
3. able to perform the procedures and maneuvers included in the standards at a more precise level than that required at the sport pilot level; and
4. competent to pass the required practical test for the issuance of the Flight Instructor Certificate—Sport Pilot with the associated category/class privilege or the addition of a category/class privileges at the Flight Instructor Certificate.

Throughout the flight instructor applicant's training, the flight instructor is responsible for emphasizing the performance of, and the ability to teach, effective visual scanning, runway incursion avoidance, and collision avoidance procedures. The flight instructor applicant should develop and use scenario based teaching methods particularly on special emphasis areas. These areas are covered in AC 90-48, Pilot's Role in Collision Avoidance; FAA-H-8083-3, Airplane Flying Handbook; FAA-H-8083-13, Glider Flying Handbook; FAA-H-8083-21, Rotorcraft Flying Handbook; FAA-H-8083-23, Seaplane, Skiplane and Float/Ski Equipped Helicopter Handbook; FAA-H-8083-25, Pilot's Handbook of Aeronautical Knowledge; and the current Aeronautical Information Manual.

Examiner Responsibility

The examiner conducting the practical test or the authorized instructor conducting the proficiency check is responsible for determining that the applicant meets acceptable standards of teaching ability, knowledge, and skill in the selected TASKs. The examiner or authorized instructor makes this determination by accomplishing an Objective that is appropriate to each selected TASK, and includes an evaluation of the applicant's:

1. ability to apply the fundamentals of instructing;
2. knowledge of, and ability to teach, the subject matter, procedures, and maneuvers covered in the TASKs;
3. ability to perform the procedures and maneuvers included in the standards at a more precise level than that indicated in the sport pilot tolerances; and
4. ability to describe, recognize, analyze, and correct common errors related to the skill procedures and maneuvers covered in the TASKs.

It is intended that oral questioning be used at any time during the ground or flight portion of the practical test or proficiency check to determine that the applicant can instruct effectively and has a comprehensive knowledge of the TASKs and their related safety factors.

During the flight portion of the practical test or proficiency check, the examiner or authorized instructor shall act as a student during selected maneuvers. This will give the examiner or authorized instructor an opportunity to evaluate the flight instructor applicant's ability to analyze and correct simulated common errors related to these maneuvers. The examiner or authorized instructor will place special emphasis on the applicant's use of visual scanning and collision avoidance procedures, and the applicant's ability to teach those procedures.

Examiners or authorized instructors should, to the greatest extent possible, test the applicant's application and correlation skills. When possible, scenario based questions should be used during the practical test or proficiency check.

Change 1 (6/9/06)

If the examiner or authorized instructor determines that a TASK is incomplete, or the outcome uncertain, the examiner or authorized instructor, may require the applicant to repeat that TASK, or portions of that TASK. This provision has been made in the interest of fairness and does not mean that instruction, practice or the repeating of an unsatisfactory TASK is permitted during the certification process. When practical, the remaining TASKs of the practical test or proficiency check phase should be completed before repeating the questionable TASK.

Initial Flight Instructor Certification Check—Satisfactory Performance

An applicant who seeks initial flight instructor certification will be evaluated in all AREAS OF OPERATION of the standards appropriate to the category/class rating(s) sought. The examiner shall refer to the examiner's practical test checklist, for the appropriate category, located in this section, to determine the TASKs to be tested, in each AREA OF OPERATION.

The practical test is passed if, in the judgment of the examiner, the applicant demonstrates satisfactory performance with regard to:

1. knowledge of the fundamentals of instructing;
2. knowledge of the technical subject areas;
3. knowledge of the flight instructor's responsibilities concerning the pilot certification process;
4. knowledge of the flight instructor's responsibilities concerning logbook entries and pilot certificate endorsements;
5. ability to perform the procedures and maneuvers included in the standards at a more precise level than that indicated in the sport pilot tolerances while giving effective instruction;
6. competence in teaching the procedures and maneuvers selected by the examiner;
7. competence in describing, recognizing, analyzing, and correcting common errors simulated by the examiner; and
8. knowledge of the development and effective use of a course of training, a syllabus, and a lesson plan.

Initial Flight Instructor Certification Check—Unsatisfactory Performance

If, in the judgment of the examiner, the applicant does not meet the standards of performance of any TASK performed, the applicable AREA OF OPERATION is considered unsatisfactory and therefore, the practical test is failed. The examiner or applicant may discontinue the test at any time when the failure of an AREA OF OPERATION makes the applicant ineligible for the certificate sought. **The test will be continued only with the consent of the applicant.**

If the test is discontinued, the applicant is entitled credit for only those AREAS OF OPERATION and their associated TASKs satisfactorily performed. However, during the retest and at the discretion of the examiner, any TASK may be re-evaluated, including those previously considered satisfactory.

Specific reasons for disqualification is:

1. failure to perform a procedure or maneuver at a more precise level than that indicated in the sport pilot tolerances while giving effective flight instruction;
2. failure to provide an effective instructional explanation while demonstrating a procedure or maneuver (explanation during the demonstration must be clear, concise, technically accurate, and complete with no prompting from the examiner);
3. any action or lack of action by the applicant which requires corrective intervention by the examiner to maintain safe flight; or
4. failure to use proper and effective visual scanning techniques to clear the area before and while performing maneuvers.

When a Disapproval Notice is issued, the examiner shall record the applicant's unsatisfactory performance in terms of AREA(s) OF OPERATION and specific TASK(s) not meeting the standard appropriate to the practical test conducted. If the applicant fails the practical test because of a special emphasis area, the Notice of Disapproval shall indicate the associated TASK. An example would be: AREA OF OPERATION VI, Traffic Patterns, failure to teach proper collision avoidance procedures.

Proficiency Check—Satisfactory Performance When Adding an Additional Category/Class Privilege

The authorized instructor shall refer to the instructor's proficiency check checklist, for the appropriate category, located in this section, to determine the TASKs to be tested, in each AREA OF OPERATION. The proficiency check is passed if, in the judgment of the authorized instructor, the applicant demonstrates satisfactory performance with regard to:

1. knowledge of the fundamentals of instructing;
2. knowledge of the technical subject areas;
3. knowledge of the flight instructor's responsibilities concerning the pilot certification process;
4. knowledge of the flight instructor's responsibilities concerning logbook entries and pilot certificate endorsements;
5. be able to perform the procedures and maneuvers included in the standards at a more precise level than that indicated in the sport pilot tolerances while giving effective instruction;

6. competence in teaching the procedures and maneuvers selected by the examiner;
7. competence in describing, recognizing, analyzing, and correcting common errors simulated by the examiner; and
8. knowledge of the development and effective use of a course of training, a syllabus, and a lesson plan.

When an applicant is adding a category/class privileges to their Flight Instructor Certificate, the evaluating authorized instructor shall, upon successful completion of the proficiency check, endorse the applicant's logbook indicating that the applicant is qualified to instruct in an additional sport pilot category/class of aircraft. The authorized instructor shall forward FAA Form 8710-11 to Airman Registry within 10 days.

Proficiency Check—Unsatisfactory Performance When Adding an Additional Category/Class Privilege

When the applicant's performance does not meet the standard in the PTS, the authorized instructor conducting the proficiency check shall annotate the unsatisfactory performance on the FAA Form 8710-11 and forward it to Airman Registry within 10 days. A Notice of Disapproval will **NOT** be issued in this instance; rather, the applicant should be provided with a list of the AREAS OF OPERATION and the specific TASKs not meeting the standard, so that the applicant may receive additional training.

Specific reasons for disqualification is:

1. failure to perform a procedure or maneuver at a more precise level than that indicated in the sport pilot tolerances while giving effective flight instruction;
2. failure to provide an effective instructional explanation while demonstrating a procedure or maneuver (explanation during the demonstration must be clear, concise, technically accurate, and complete with no prompting from the authorized instructor);
3. any action or lack of action by the applicant which requires corrective intervention by the examiner to maintain safe flight; or
4. failure to use proper and effective visual scanning techniques to clear the area before and while performing maneuvers.

When the applicant receives the additional training in the AREAS OF OPERATION and the specific TASK(s) found deficient during the proficiency check, the recommending instructor shall endorse the applicant's logbook indicating that the applicant has received additional instruction and has been found competent to pass the proficiency check. The applicant shall complete a new FAA Form 8710-11, and the recommending instructor shall endorse the application. The authorized instructor, other than the one who provided the additional training, shall evaluate the applicant. When the applicant successfully accomplishes a complete proficiency check, the authorized instructor, shall forward the FAA Form 8710-11 to Airman Registry within 10 days and indorse the applicant's logbook indicating the airman's additional privileges.

Renewal or Reinstatement of a Flight Instructor Certificate

14 CFR part 61, sections 61.197(a) (1) and 61.199(a) allow an individual that holds a Flight Instructor Certificate to renew or reinstate that certificate by passing a practical test. The examiner shall develop a plan of action that includes at least one TASK, in each AREA OF OPERATION, in the examiner's practical test checklist, for the appropriate category, located in this section. The Renewal or Reinstatement of one rating on a Flight Instructor Certificate renews or reinstates all privileges existing on the certificate.

I. AREA OF OPERATION: FUNDAMENTALS OF INSTRUCTING

NOTE: The examiner shall select TASK F and one other TASK.

A. TASK: THE LEARNING PROCESS

REFERENCE: FAA-H-8083-9.

Objective. To determine that the applicant exhibits instructional knowledge of the elements of the learning process by describing:

1. Learning theory.
2. Characteristics of learning.
3. Principles of learning.
4. Levels of learning.
5. Learning physical skills.
6. Memory.
7. Transfer of learning.

B. TASK: HUMAN BEHAVIOR AND EFFECTIVE COMMUNICATION

REFERENCE: FAA-H-8083-9.

Objective. To determine that the applicant exhibits instructional knowledge of the elements of the teaching process by describing:

1. Human behavior—

    a. control of human behavior.
    b. human needs.
    c. defense mechanisms.
    d. the flight instructor as a practical psychologist.

2. Effective communication—

    a. basic elements of communication.
    b. barriers of effective communication.
    c. developing communication skills.

C. TASK: THE TEACHING PROCESS

REFERENCE: FAA-H-8083-9.

Objective.   To determine that the applicant exhibits instructional knowledge of the elements of the teaching process by describing:

1. Preparation of a lesson for a ground or flight instructional period.
2. Presentation methods.
3. Application, by the student, of the material or procedure presented.
4. Review and evaluation of student performance.

D. TASK: TEACHING METHODS

REFERENCE: FAA-H-8083-9.

Objective.   To determine that the applicant exhibits instructional knowledge of the elements of teaching methods by describing:

1. Material organization.
2. The lecture method.
3. The cooperative or group learning method.
4. The guided discussion method.
5. The demonstration-performance method.
6. Computer-based training method.

E. TASK: CRITIQUE AND EVALUATION

REFERENCE: FAA-H-8083-9.

Objective.   To determine that the applicant exhibits instructional knowledge of the elements of critique and evaluation by explaining:

1. Critique—

    a. purpose and characteristics of an effective critique.
    b. methods and ground rules for a critique.

2. Evaluation—

    a. characteristics of effective oral questions and what types to avoid.
    b. responses to student questions.
    c. characteristics and development of effective written questions.
    d. characteristics and uses of performance test, specifically, the FAA practical test standards.

F. TASK: FLIGHT INSTRUCTOR CHARACTERISTICS AND RESPONSIBILITIES

REFERENCE: FAA-H-8083-9.

Objective. To determine that the applicant exhibits instructional knowledge of the elements of flight instructor characteristics and responsibilities by describing:

1. Aviation instructor responsibilities in—

   a. providing adequate instruction.
   b. establishing standards of performance.
   c. emphasizing the positive.
   d. develop plans of action for use during proficiency checks.
   e. completion of FAA Form 8710-11.

2. Flight instructor responsibilities in—

   a. providing student pilot evaluation and supervision.
   b. preparing practical test recommendations and endorsements.
   c. determining requirements for conducting additional training and endorsement requirements.
   d. conducting proficiency checks for additional category/class privileges.

3. Professionalism as an instructor by—

   a. explaining important personal characteristics.
   b. describing methods to minimize student frustration.

G. TASK: PLANNING INSTRUCTIONAL ACTIVITY

REFERENCE: FAA-H-8083-9.

Objective. To determine that the applicant exhibits instructional knowledge of the elements of planning instructional activity by describing:

1. Developing objectives and standards for a course of training.
2. Theory of building blocks of learning.
3. Requirements for developing a training syllabus.
4. Purpose and characteristics of a lesson plan.

II. AREA OF OPERATION: TECHNICAL SUBJECT AREAS

NOTE: The examiner shall select TASK D and at least one other TASK.

A. TASK: AEROMEDICAL FACTORS

REFERENCES: FAA-H-8083-3, FAA-S-8081-12, FAA-S-8081-14; AIM.

Objective. To determine that the applicant exhibits instructional knowledge of the elements related to aeromedical factors by describing:

1. How to obtain an appropriate medical certificate.
2. How to obtain a medical certificate in the event of a possible medical deficiency.
3. The causes, symptoms, effects, and corrective action of the following medical factors—

   a. hypoxia.
   b. hyperventilation.
   c. middle ear and sinus problems.
   d. spatial disorientation.
   e. motion sickness.
   f. carbon monoxide poisoning.
   g. fatigue and stress.
   h. dehydration.
   i. hypothermia.

4. The effects of alcohol and drugs, and their relationship to flight safety.
5. The effect of nitrogen excesses incurred during scuba dives and how this affects pilots and passengers during flight.

B. TASK: VISUAL SCANNING AND COLLISION AVOIDANCE

REFERENCES: FAA-H-8083-3, FAA-H-8083-25; AC 90-48; AIM.

Objective.   To determine that the applicant exhibits instructional knowledge of the elements of visual scanning and collision avoidance by describing:

1. Relationship between a pilot's physical condition and vision.
2. Environmental conditions that degrade vision.
3. Vestibular and visual illusions.
4. "See and avoid" concept.
5. Proper visual scanning procedures.
6. Relationship between poor visual scanning habits and increased collision risk.
7. Proper clearing procedures.
8. Importance of knowing aircraft blind spots.
9. Relationship between aircraft speed differential and collision risk.
10. Situations that involve the greatest collision risk.

C. TASK: FEDERAL AVIATION REGULATIONS AND PUBLICATIONS

REFERENCES: 14 CFR parts 1, 61, 91; NTSB part 830; AC 00-2; FAA-H-8083-25; Aircraft Flight Manual/POH; AIM.

Objective.   To determine that the applicant exhibits instructional knowledge of the elements related to the Code of Federal Regulations and publications:

1. Availability and method of revision of 14 CFR parts 1, 61, 91, and NTSB part 830 by describing—

    a. purpose.
    b. general content.

2. Availability of flight information publications, advisory circulars, practical test standards, pilot operating handbooks, and FAA-approved aircraft flight manuals by describing—

    a. availability.
    b. purpose.
    c. general content.

D. TASK: LOGBOOK ENTRIES AND CERTIFICATE
ENDORSEMENTS

REFERENCES: 14 CFR part 61; AC 61-65.

Objective.   To determine that the applicant exhibits instructional knowledge of the elements related to logbook entries and certificate endorsements by describing:

1. Required logbook entries for instruction given.
2. Required student pilot certificate endorsements, including appropriate logbook entries.
3. Preparation of a recommendation for a pilot practical test/ proficiency check, including appropriate logbook entry for—

   a. initial pilot certification.
   b. additional pilot certification.
   c. additional aircraft category/class privileges.
   d. make and model privileges.
   e. single-seat aircraft.

4. Required endorsement of a pilot logbook for the satisfactory completion of the required FAA flight review/proficiency check.
5. Required flight instructor records.

III. AREA OF OPERATION: PREFLIGHT LESSON ON A MANEUVER TO BE PERFORMED IN FLIGHT

NOTE: Examiner shall select at least one maneuver TASK, and ask the applicant to present a preflight lesson on the selected maneuver as the lesson would be taught to a student.

A. TASK: MANEUVER LESSON

REFERENCE: FAA-S-8081-12, FAA-S-8081-14; FAA-H-8083-3, FAA-H-8083-9, FAA-H-8083-13, FAA-H-8083-21, FAA-H-8083-25; Glider Flight Manual/POH.

Objective. To determine that the applicant exhibits instructional knowledge of the selected maneuver by:

1. Stating the purpose.
2. Giving an accurate, comprehensive oral description including the elements and common errors.
3. Using instructional aids, as appropriate.
4. Describing the recognition, analysis, and correction of common errors.

Note: Refer to the appropriate checklist for those the additional items that must be tested in section 1 of the PTS.

U.S. Department
of Transportation

**Federal Aviation
Administration**

FAA-S-8081-31
with Changes 1 and 2

SPORT PILOT

Practical Test Standards

for

- # Weight Shift Control
  - # Powered Parachute
    - # Flight Instructor

December 2004

FLIGHT STANDARDS SERVICE
Washington, DC 20591

SPORT PILOT

Practical Test Standards

2004

FLIGHT STANDARDS SERVICE
Washington, DC 20591

NOTE

Material in FAA-S-8081-31 will be effective December 2004.

Record of Changes

Change 1—6/9/2006

1. Deleted the additional category/class matrix; applicants for an additional category/class privileges must take a complete practical test.
2. Added weather elements for inadvertent entry into IMC on pages 1-2 and 2-2.
3. Deleted the ATC light signal requirements from airport operations page 1-10 and 2-9.
4. Deleted all references to repositionable landing gear, multiple pages.
5. Deleted energy management TASK, page 1-20, for weight shift control and added an energy management element to emergency approach and landing for weight shift control, page 1-26.
6. Added line-over and twisted suspension line elements to powered parachute canopy layout page 2-6.
7. Changed testing requirements of taxiing with the canopy inflated in a powered parachute, from flight instructors only, to sport pilots and flight instructors with a sport pilot rating, page 2-7.
8. Added heading tolerances (±10°) to constant altitude turns for powered parachute.
9. Added proficiency check materials to flight instructor characteristics and responsibilities page 3-15.
10. Created category specific examiner/instructor checklists for the flight instructor with a sport pilot rating pages 3-v – 3-xx to replace the flight instructor matrix.
11. Deleted the flight instructor matrixes. See above.

Change 2—02/22/2008

1. Global: changed all "AFM" to Aircraft Flight Manual."
2. Page 4: added Advisory Circulars to the reference list for emergency equipment.
3. Page 4: list of References for Practical Test Standards, added "Aircraft Flight Manual."
4. Page 4: list of Abbreviations, deleted "AFM." The name of the aircraft is now always spelled out—no acronyms.
5. Page 5: list of Abbreviations: added PPLC, Powered Parachute—Land; PPCS, Powered Parachute—Sea; WSCL, Weight Shift Controlled—Land; WSCS, Weight Shift Controlled—Sea.
6. Global in Section 1—Weight Shift Control references: changed "AFM" to "Aircraft Flight Manual."
7. Global under Section 1 references: replaced "AFM" with "Aircraft Flight Manual."
8. Page 1-viii: IX (Emergency Operations): deleted "Power-off approach and accuracy landing." The task is not in the PTS.

9. Page 1-1: I (Preflight Preparation), A (Certificates and Documents), Objective 2 (determining applicant knowledge of the elements related to certificates and documents by), b. (locating and explaining): added "Aircraft Flight Manual/POH."

10. Page 1-1: I (Preflight Preparation), B (Airworthiness Requirements), Objective 1a. (explaining "required instruments and equipment for sport pilot privileges"): added "(as required by the operating limitations)."

11. Page 1-1: deleted Objective 1c.: (explaining) "requirements and procedures for obtaining a special flight permit."

12. Pages 1-2 and 2-2: C (Weather Information), References: added "FAA-H-8083-3" to address inadvertent flight into IMC.

13. Page 1-23: VII (Navigation) A (Pilotage and Dead Reckoning) Objective 4 ("Verifies the aircraft's position with 3 nautical miles of the flight-planned route"): changed "with" to "within."

14. Page 1-27: C (Emergency Equipment and Survival Gear (WSCL and WSCS)) References: deleted "FAA-H-8083-23" and "FAA-H-8083-25"; added "AC 91-13," "AC 91-58," and "AC 91-69."

15. Page 1-28: X (Postflight Procedures) B (Anchoring), Objectives 2 and 3: changed "seaplane" to "aircraft."

16. Page 1-29: C (Docking and Mooring (WSCS)) Objective 3, and D (Ramping/Beaching (WSCA)) Objective 3 : changed "seaplane" to "aircraft."

17. Global in Section 2 —Powered Parachute references, except in those sections referring to PPCS only: added "FAA-H-8083-29."

18. Global in Section 2 references: deleted all references to "PPC Training Manual."

19. Page 2-1: Renumbered the elements under Task B Airworthiness Requirements.

20. Page 2-1: Task B Airworthiness Requirements, Element 1. a., added "(as required by the operating limitations)."

21. Page 2-1: Task B Airworthiness Requirements, deleted element 1.c., "requirements and procedures for obtaining a special flight permit."

22. Page 2-4: deleted element 2. c., carbon monoxide poisoning, from Task G, Aeromedical Factors.

23. Page 2-4: H: replaced "seaplane" with "powered parachute—sea" in both task title and Objective. In task H, Objective 2: changed "seaplane" to "aircraft."

24. Page 2-9: B (Traffic Patterns (PPCL and PPCS) Objective (determining that applicant) "Exhibits knowledge of the elements related to radio communications airports without operating control towers": inserted "at" between "communications" and "airports."

25. Page 2-16: Added a heading tolerance to constant altitude turns "and rolls out on the entry heading ±10°."

26. Page 2-20: deleted "rotor/and or" from Task B (systems and equipment malfunctions), element 2.f., from powered parachute.

27. Page 2-21: added references to emergency equipment and survival gear task: "AC 91-13, AC 91-58, AC 91-69" and "AIM."
28. Page 3-vii: added bold font to mandatory tasks on page 3-vii.
29. Page 3-viii: corrected the examiner note under the emergency operations area of operations ("The examiner must select TASK A"), by adding "and one other TASK for WSC."
30. Page 3-viii: deleted Task option "B. Power-off approach and accuracy landing."
31. Page 3-xi: added bold font to mandatory tasks.
32. Page 3-xii: corrected the examiner note under the emergency operations area of operations.
33. Page 3-xvii and 3-xviii: added bold font to mandatory tasks.

FOREWORD

The Sport Pilot Practical Test Standards for Weight Shift Control, Powered Parachute, and Flight Instructor has been published by the Federal Aviation Administration (FAA) to establish the standards for the knowledge and skills necessary for the issuance of a Sport Pilot Certificate and a Flight Instructor Certificate with a Sport Pilot Rating.

FAA inspectors, designated pilot examiners, and flight instructors shall conduct instruction, proficiency checks, and practical tests in compliance with these standards. Flight instructors and applicants should find these standards helpful during training and when preparing for the practical test or proficiency check.

/s/ 12-20-2004
_____

Joseph K. Tintera, Manager
Regulatory Support Division
Flight Standards Service

CONTENTS

AREAS OF OPERATION

Section 2—SPORT PILOT POWERED PARACHUTE

CONTENTS

CHECKLISTS

AREAS OF OPERATION

SECTION 3—SPORT PILOT FLIGHT INSTRUCTOR

CONTENTS

CHECKLISTS

FLIGHT INSTRUCTOR CERTIFICATE WITH SPORT PILOT PRIVILEGES

AREAS OF OPERATION

INTRODUCTION

General Information

The Flight Standards Service of the Federal Aviation Administration (FAA) has developed this practical test book as the standard that must be used by FAA inspectors and designated pilot examiners (DPEs), when conducting sport pilot and flight instructor with a sport pilot rating practical tests or proficiency checks.

The word "examiner" is used throughout the standards to denote either the FAA inspector or an FAA designated pilot examiner who conducts an official practical test or proficiency check. When an examiner conducts a proficiency check they are acting in the capacity of an authorized instructor.

A proficiency check is an evaluation of aeronautical knowledge and flight proficiency IAW Title 14 of the Code of Federal Regulations (14 CFR) part 61, section 61.321 or 61.419. A proficiency check must be administered using the appropriate practical test standard (PTS) for the category of aircraft when a pilot or a flight instructor adds new category/class privileges. Upon successful completion of the proficiency check the authorized instructor will endorse the applicant's logbook indicating the added category/class of equipment that the applicant is authorized to operate. When an examiner conducts a proficiency check they are acting in the capacity of an authorized instructor.

DPEs must have designation authority to conduct sport pilot initial evaluations (Sport Pilot Examiner [SPE]) and flight instructor with a sport pilot rating initial evaluations (Sport Pilot Flight Instructor Examiner [SFIE]) per FAA Order 8710.7, Sport Pilot Examiner's Handbook.

Authorized instructors must use this PTS when preparing applicants for practical tests or proficiency checks and when conducting proficiency checks. Applicants should be familiar with this book and refer to these standards during their training.

Information considered directive in nature is described in this practical test book in terms, such as "shall" and "must" indicating the actions are mandatory. Guidance information is described in terms, such as "should" and "may" indicating the actions are desirable or permissive, but not mandatory.

The FAA gratefully acknowledges the valuable assistance provided by many individuals and organizations throughout the aviation community who contributed their time and talent in assisting with the development of this practical test standard.

This PTS may be purchased from the Superintendent of Documents, U.S. Government Printing Office (GPO), Washington, DC 20402-9325, or from http://bookstore.gpo.gov. This PTS is also available for download, in pdf format, from the Flight Standards Service web site at www.faa.gov.

The U.S. Department of Transportation, Federal Aviation Administration, Airman Testing Standards Branch, AFS-630, P.O. BOX 25082, Oklahoma City, OK 73125 publishes this PTS. Comments regarding this PTS should be sent, in e-mail form, to AFS630comments@faa.gov.

Practical Test Standards Concept

14 CFR part 61.311 specifies the AREAS OF OPERATION in which knowledge and skill must be demonstrated by the applicant before the issuance of a Sport Pilot Certificate or privileges. The CFRs provide the flexibility to permit the FAA to publish practical test standards containing the AREAS OF OPERATION and specific TASKs in which pilot competency must be demonstrated. The FAA must revise this practical test standard whenever it is determined that changes are needed in the interest of safety. **Adherence to the provisions of the regulations and the practical test standards is mandatory for practical tests and proficiency checks.**

Practical Test Book Description

This test book contains the following Sport Pilot Practical Test Standards.

Section 1—Weight Shift Control
Section 2—Powered Parachute
Section 3—Flight Instructor (The flight instructor section contains a separate introduction in section 3.)

The Sport Pilot Practical Test Standards include the AREAS OF OPERATION and TASKs for the issuance of an initial Sport Pilot Certificate and for the addition of sport pilot category/class privileges. It also contains information on how to obtain an initial Flight Instructor Certificate with a sport pilot rating and for the addition of flight instructor category/class privileges.

Practical Test Standards Description

AREAS OF OPERATION are phases of the practical test or proficiency check arranged in a logical sequence within each standard. They begin with Preflight Preparation and end with Postflight Procedures. The examiner may conduct the practical test or proficiency check in any sequence that will result in a complete and efficient test. An authorized instructor may conduct a proficiency check in any sequence that will result in a complete and efficient test. **However, the ground portion of the practical test or proficiency check must be accomplished before the flight portion.**

TASKs are specific knowledge areas, flight procedures, or maneuvers appropriate to an AREA OF OPERATION. The abbreviation(s) within parentheses immediately following a TASK refer to the appropriate class of aircraft. The meaning of each class abbreviation is as follows:

WSCL Weight Shift Control—Land
WSCS Weight Shift Control—Sea
PPCL Powered Parachute—Land
PPCS Powered Parachute—Sea

When administering a test using section 1, 2, or 3 of this PTS, the TASKs appropriate to the class aircraft (WSCL, WSCS, PPCL, and PPCS) used for the test must be included in the plan of action. The absence of a class indicates the TASK is for all classes.

NOTE is used to emphasize special considerations required in the AREA OF OPERATION or TASK.

REFERENCE identifies the publication(s) that describe(s) the TASK. Descriptions of TASKs are not included in these standards because this information can be found in the current issue of the listed reference. Publications other than those listed may be used for reference if their content conveys substantially the same meaning as the referenced publications.

These practical test standards are based on the following references.

14 CFR part 43	Maintenance, Preventive Maintenance, Rebuilding, and Alteration
14 CFR part 61	Certification: Pilots, Flight Instructors, and Ground Instructors
14 CFR part 67	Medical Standards Certification
14 CFR part 71	Designation of class A, B, C, D, and E airspace
14 CFR part 91	General Operating and Flight Rules
AC 00-6	Aviation Weather
AC 00-45	Aviation Weather Services
AC 60-22	Aeronautical Decision Making

AC 60-28	English Language Skill Standards
AC 61-65	Certification: Pilot and Flight Instructors and Ground Instructors
AC 61-67	Stall and Spin Awareness Training
AC 61-84	Role of Preflight Preparation
AC 61-134	General Aviation Controlled Flight Into Terrain Awareness
AC 90-23	Aircraft Wake Turbulence
AC 90-48	Pilots' Role in Collision Avoidance
AC 90-66	Recommended Standard Traffic Patterns and Practices for Aeronautical Operations At Airports Without Operating Control Towers
AC 91-69	Seaplane Safety for FAR Part 91 Operations
AC 120-51	Crew Resource Management Training
FAA-H-8083-1	Aircraft Weight and Balance Handbook
FAA-H-8083-3	Airplane Flying Handbook
FAA-H-8083-9	Aviation Instructor's Handbook
FAA-H-8083-13	Glider Flying Handbook
FAA-H-8083-15	Instrument Flying Handbook
FAA-H-8083-23	Seaplane, Skiplane, and Float/Ski Equipped Helicopter Flying Handbook
FAA-H-8083-25	Pilot's Handbook of Aeronautical Knowledge
AIM	Aeronautical Information Manual
AFD	Airport/Facility Directory
AFM	Aircraft Flight Manual
NOTAMs	Notices to Airmen
Other	Pilot Operating Handbook/ FAA-Approved Flight Manual Aeronautical Navigation Charts Seaplane Supplement Powered Parachute Bible Weight Shift Control Aviation Handbook

The Objective lists the important elements that must be satisfactorily performed to demonstrate competency in a TASK. The Objective includes:

1. specifically what the applicant should be able to do;
2. conditions under which the TASK is to be performed;
3. acceptable performance standards; and
4. safety considerations, when applicable.

Abbreviations

14 CFR	Title 14 of the Code of Federal Regulations
AC	Advisory Circular
ADM	Aeronautical Decision Making
AFD	Airport Facility Directory
AFSS	Automated Flight Service Station
AGL	Above Ground Level

AIM	Aeronautical Information Manual
ASEL	Airplane Single Engine—Land
ASES	Airplane Single Engine—Sea
ASOS	Automated Surface Observing System
ATC	Air Traffic Control
ATIS	Automatic Terminal Information Service
AWOS	Automated Weather Observing System
CFIT	Controlled Flight into Terrain
CRM	Cockpit Resource Management
CTAF	Common Traffic Advisory Frequency
FA	Area Weather Forecast
FAA	Federal Aviation Administration
GPO	Government Printing Office
IMC	Instrument Meteorological Conditions
METAR	Meteorological Aviation Report (Routine)
NOTAM	Notices to Airmen
NTSB	National Transportation Safety Board
POH	Pilot Operating Handbook
PPC	Powered Parachute
PPCL	Powered Parachute—Land
PPCS	Powered Parachute—Sea
PTS	Practical Test Standard
RPM	Revolutions per Minute
SS	Single-Seat
SUA	Special Use Airspace
TAF	Terminal Aviation Forecast
TFR	Temporary Flight Restrictions
VFR	Visual Flight Rules
WSC	Weight-Shift Control
WSCL	Weight-Shift Control—Land
WSCS	Weight-Shift Control—Sea

Use of the Practical Test Standards Book

The FAA requires that all sport pilot and sport pilot flight instructor practical tests and proficiency checks be conducted in accordance with the appropriate sport pilot practical test standards and the policies set forth in this INTRODUCTION. Applicants must be evaluated in **ALL** TASKs included in each AREA OF OPERATION of the appropriate practical test standard, unless otherwise noted.

An applicant, who holds at least a Sport Pilot Certificate seeking additional aircraft category/class privileges at the sport pilot level, must be evaluated in all the AREAS OF OPERATION and TASKs listed in the PTS.

In preparation for each practical test or proficiency check, the examiner or authorized instructor must develop a written "plan of action." The "plan of action" must include all TASKs in each AREA OF OPERATION, unless noted otherwise. If the elements in one TASK have already been evaluated in another TASK, they need not be repeated.

For example, the "plan of action" need not include evaluating the applicant on complying with markings at the end of the flight, if that element was sufficiently observed at the beginning of the flight. **Any TASK selected for evaluation during a practical test or proficiency check must be evaluated in its entirety.** Exception: examiners evaluating single-seat applicants from the ground must evaluate only those TASK **elements** that can be accurately assessed from the ground.

The examiner or authorized instructor is not required to follow the precise order in which the AREAS OF OPERATION and TASKs appear in this book. The examiner or authorized instructor may change the sequence or combine TASKs with similar Objectives to have an orderly and efficient flow of the practical test or proficiency check events.

The examiner's or authorized instructor's "plan of action" must include the order and combination of TASKs to be demonstrated by the applicant in a manner that will result in an efficient and valid test.

The examiner or authorized instructor is expected to use good judgment in the performance of simulated emergency procedures. The use of the safest means for simulation is expected. Consideration must be given to local conditions, both meteorological and topographical, at the time of the test, as well as the applicant's workload, and the condition of the aircraft used during the practical test or proficiency check. **If the procedure being evaluated would jeopardize safety, it is expected that the applicant will simulate that portion of the maneuver.**

Special Emphasis Areas

Examiners and authorized instructors must place special emphasis upon areas of aircraft operations considered critical to flight safety. Among these are:

1. positive aircraft control;
2. procedures for positive exchange of flight controls;
3. stall and spin awareness (if appropriate);
4. collision avoidance;
5. wake turbulence and low level wind shear avoidance;
6. runway incursion avoidance;
7. controlled flight into terrain (CFIT);
8. aeronautical decision making/risk management;
9. checklist usage;
10. spatial disorientation;
11. temporary flight restrictions (TFR);
12. special use airspace (SUA);
13. aviation security; and
14. other areas deemed appropriate to any phase of the practical test or proficiency check.

Although these areas may not be specifically addressed under each TASK, they are essential to flight safety and will be evaluated during the practical test or proficiency check. In all instances, the applicant's actions will be evaluated in accordance to the standards of the TASKs and the ability to use good judgment with reference to the special emphasis areas listed above.

Sport Pilot—Practical Test Prerequisites (Initial)

An applicant for a Sport Pilot Certificate is required by 14 CFR part 61 to:

1. be at least 17 years of age (or 16 if applying to operate a glider or balloon);
2. be able to read, speak, write, and understand the English language. If there is a doubt, use AC 60-28, English Language Skill Standards;
3. have passed the appropriate sport pilot knowledge test since the beginning of the 24th month before the month in which he or she takes a practical test;
4. have satisfactorily accomplished the required training and obtained the aeronautical experience prescribed;
5. possess a current and valid U.S. driver's license or a valid Airman Medical Certificate issued under 14 CFR part 67;
6. have an endorsement from an authorized instructor certifying that the applicant has received and logged training time within 60 days preceding the date of application in preparation for the practical test, and is prepared for the practical test; and
7. have an endorsement certifying that the applicant has demonstrated satisfactory knowledge of the subject areas in which the applicant was deficient on the airman knowledge test.

Sport Pilot—Practical Test Prerequisites (Registered Ultra-Light Pilots)

If you are a registered ultra-light pilot with an FAA-recognized ultra-light organization on or before September 1, 2004, and you want to apply for a Sport Pilot Certificate, then you must, not later than January 31, 2007 (14 CFR part 61, section 61.329):

1. meet the eligibility requirements in 14 CFR part 61, sections 61.305 and 61.23, but **not** the aeronautical knowledge requirements specified in section 61.309 , the flight proficiency requirements specified in section 61.311, and the aeronautical experience requirements specified in section 61.313;
2. pass the knowledge test for a Sport Pilot Certificate specified in 14 CFR part 61, section 61.307 or the knowledge test for a Flight Instructor Certificate with a sport pilot rating specified in section 61.405;
3. pass the practical test for a Sport Pilot Certificate specified in 14 CFR part 61, section 61.307;

4. provide the FAA with a certified copy of your ultra-light pilot records from an FAA-recognized ultra-light organization, and those records must—

    a. document that you are a registered ultra-light pilot with that FAA-recognized ultra-light organization; and

    b. indicate that you are recognized to operate each category and class of aircraft for which you seek sport pilot privileges.

Sport Pilot—Additional Privileges

If you hold a Sport Pilot Certificate or higher and seek to operate an additional category or class of light-sport aircraft (14 CFR part 61, section 61.321), you must:

1. receive a logbook endorsement from the authorized instructor who trained you on the applicable aeronautical knowledge areas specified in 14 CFR part 61, section 61.309 and areas of operation specified in section 61.311. The endorsement certifies you have met the aeronautical knowledge and flight proficiency requirements for the additional light-sport aircraft privileges you seek;

2. successfully complete a proficiency check from an authorized instructor other than the one who trained you on the aeronautical knowledge areas and areas of operation specified in 14 CFR part 61, sections 61.309 and 61.311 for the additional light-sport aircraft privilege you seek;

3. complete an application for those privileges on a form in a manner acceptable to the FAA and present this application to the authorized instructor who conducted the proficiency check specified in above paragraph;

4. receive a logbook endorsement from the instructor who conducted the proficiency check specified in 2 above, certifying you are proficient in the applicable areas of operation and aeronautical knowledge areas and that you are authorized for the additional category and class light-sport aircraft privilege.

Aircraft and Equipment Required for the Practical Test/Proficiency Check

The applicant for a Sport Pilot Certificate is required in accordance with 14 CFR part 61, section 61.45, to provide an aircraft that has a current airworthiness certificate and is in a condition for safe flight, for use during the practical test or proficiency check. This section further requires that the aircraft must:

1. be of U.S., foreign or military registry of the same category, class, and type, if applicable, for the certificate or privileges for which the applicant is applying;
2. have fully functioning dual controls, except as provided for in 14 CFR part 61, section 61.45(c), (e), and (f);
3. be capable of performing all AREAS OF OPERATION appropriate to the privileges sought and have no operating limitations, which prohibit its use in any of the AREAS OF OPERATION, required for the practical test or proficiency check; and
4. have an altitude and an airspeed indicating system, as appropriate, for all tasks that require demonstration of skill within an altitude/airspeed tolerance.

The aircraft utilized for sport pilot and sport pilot flight instructor practical tests and proficiency checks must be a light-sport aircraft as defined in 14 CFR part 1.

Flight Instructor Responsibility

An appropriately rated flight instructor is responsible for training the sport pilot applicant to acceptable standards in ALL subject matter areas, procedures, and maneuvers included in the TASKs within each single-seat aircraft practical test.

Because of the impact of their teaching activities in developing safe, proficient pilots, flight instructors should exhibit a high level of knowledge, skill, and the ability to impart that knowledge and skill to students.

Throughout the applicant's training, the flight instructor is responsible for emphasizing the performance of effective visual scanning and collision avoidance procedures.

Single-Seat Aircraft Practical Test

Applicants for a Sport Pilot Certificate may elect to take their test in a single-seat aircraft. The FAA established in 14 CFR part 61, section 61.45(f) specific requirements to allow a practical test for a Sport Pilot Certificate only. This provision does not allow a practical test for a Flight Instructor Certificate or Recreation Pilot Certificate or higher to be conducted in a light-sport aircraft that has a single-pilot seat.

With certain limitations, the practical test for a Sport Pilot Certificate may be conducted from the ground by an examiner. The examiner must agree to conduct the practical test in a single-seat aircraft and must ensure that the practical test is conducted in accordance with the sport pilot practical test standards for single-seat aircraft. **Knowledge of all TASKs applicable to their category/class of aircraft will be evaluated orally.** Single-seat sport pilots must demonstrate competency in those specific TASKs identified by a NOTE in the AREA OF OPERATION for a single-seat practical test and any other TASKs selected by the examiner. Examiners evaluating single-seat applicants from the ground must evaluate only those TASK **elements** that can be accurately assessed from the ground.

The examiner **must maintain radio contact** with the applicant and be in a position to observe the operation of the aircraft while evaluating the proficiency of the applicant from the ground.

Sport pilots taking the practical test in a single-seat aircraft will have the limitation, "No passenger carriage and flight in a single-pilot seat aircraft only" placed on their pilot certificate, per section 61.45(f)(3), limiting their operations to a single-seat light-sport aircraft and no passenger carriage will be authorized.

Only an examiner is authorized to remove this limitation when the sport pilot takes a complete practical test in a two-place light-sport aircraft. This practical test may be conducted in the same or additional category of aircraft.

Upon successful completion of the practical test, the limitation will be removed, and the sport pilot is authorized to act as pilot in command in all categories of light-sport aircraft that he or she has a make and model endorsement within a set of aircraft to operate. The limitation can also be removed if the sport pilot completes the certification requirements in an aircraft with a minimum of two places, for a higher certificate or rating.

Single-Seat Aircraft Proficiency Check

Sport pilot proficiency checks may by preformed in a single-seat aircraft. The FAA believes it is appropriate for an instructor to perform a proficiency check for an additional category or privilege in accordance with 14 CFR part 61, section 61.321, to be added to a Sport Pilot Certificate or higher using a single-seat light-sport aircraft, providing the authorized instructor is an examiner. When an examiner conducts a proficiency check they are acting in the capacity of an authorized instructor.

The authorized instructor must agree to conduct the practical test in a single seat light-sport aircraft and must ensure that the proficiency check is conducted in accordance with the sport pilot practical test standards for single-seat aircraft. Knowledge of all TASKs applicable to the category or class of aircraft will be evaluated orally. Those pilots seeking sport pilot privileges in a single-seat light-sport aircraft must demonstrate competency in those specific TASKs identified by a NOTE in the AREA OF OPERATION for a single-seat proficiency check and any other TASKs selected by the authorized instructor. Authorized instructors evaluating single-seat applicants from the ground must evaluate only those TASK **elements** that can be accurately assessed from the ground.

The authorized instructor must have radio contact and be in a position to observe the operation of the light-sport aircraft and evaluate the proficiency of the applicant from the ground.

On successful completion of a proficiency check, the authorized instructor will issue an endorsement with the following limitation "No passenger carriage and flight in a single-pilot seat aircraft only (add category/class/make and model)" limiting his or her operations to a single-seat aircraft in this category, class, make, and model. The authorized instructor must sign this endorsement with his or her flight instructor and examiner number.

This limitation can be removed by successfully completing a complete proficiency check, in a two-place light-sport aircraft in that specific category and class, in accordance with 14 CFR part 61, section 61.321. This proficiency check must be conducted in the same category and class of light-sport aircraft. Upon successful completion of the proficiency check, the applicant will be given an endorsement for the aircraft privilege sought.

Those recreational pilots or higher exercising sport pilot privileges will be required to have an endorsement for only the category and/or class of light-sport aircraft they are now authorized to act as pilot in command. A sport pilot will be required to have an endorsement for the category, class, make, and model within a set of aircraft in which he or she is now authorized to act as pilot in command.

Examiner Responsibility

The examiner conducting the practical test or authorized instructor conducting the proficiency check is responsible for determining that the applicant meets the acceptable standards of knowledge and skill of each TASK within each appropriate AREA OF OPERATION. Since there is no formal division between the "oral" and "skill" portions of the practical test or proficiency check, this oral portion becomes an ongoing process throughout the test. Oral questioning, to determine the applicant's knowledge of TASKs and related safety factors, should be used judiciously at all times, especially during the flight portion of the practical test or proficiency check. Examiners and authorized instructors must test to the greatest extent practicable the applicant's correlative abilities rather than mere rote enumeration of facts throughout the practical test or proficiency check.

If the examiner or authorized instructor determines that a TASK is incomplete, or the outcome uncertain, the examiner may require the applicant to repeat that TASK, or portions of that TASK. This provision has been made in the interest of fairness and does not mean that instruction, practice, or the repeating of an unsatisfactory TASK is permitted during the certification process. When practical, the remaining TASKs of the practical test or proficiency check phase should be completed before repeating the questionable TASK.

The examiner or authorized instructor must use scenarios when applicable to determine that the applicant can use good risk management procedures in making aeronautical decisions. Examples of TASKs where scenarios would be advantageous are weather analysis, performance planning, and runway/landing area selection.

Throughout the flight portion of the practical test or proficiency check, the examiner or authorized instructor must evaluate the applicant's knowledge and practical incorporation of special emphasis areas.

Initial Check—Sport Pilot-Satisfactory Performance

Satisfactory performance of TASKs to meet the requirements for sport pilot certification is based on the applicant's ability to safely:

1. perform the TASKs specified in the AREAS OF OPERATION for the certificate or privileges rating sought within the approved standards;
2. demonstrate mastery of the aircraft with the successful outcome of each TASK performed never seriously in doubt;
3. demonstrate satisfactory proficiency and competency within the approved standards;

4. demonstrate sound judgment in aeronautical decision making/ risk management; and
5. demonstrate single-pilot competence in an aircraft with a single pilot seat (if applicable).

Initial Check—Sport Pilot—Unsatisfactory Performance

The tolerances represent the performance expected in good flying conditions. If, in the judgment of the examiner, the applicant does not meet the standards of performance of any TASK performed, the associated AREA OF OPERATION is failed and therefore, the practical test is failed.

The examiner or applicant may discontinue the test at any time when the failure of an AREA OF OPERATION makes the applicant ineligible for the certificate. **The test may be continued ONLY with the consent of the applicant.**

If the test is discontinued, the applicant is entitled credit for only those AREAS OF OPERATION and their associated TASKs satisfactorily performed. However, during the retest, and at the discretion of the examiner, any TASK may be re-evaluated, including those previously passed.

The following are typical areas of unsatisfactory performance and grounds for disqualification:

1. Any action or lack of action by the applicant that requires corrective intervention by the examiner to maintain safe flight.
2. Failure to use proper and effective visual scanning techniques to clear the area before and while performing maneuvers.
3. Consistently exceeding tolerances stated in the Objectives.
4. Failure to take prompt corrective action when tolerances are exceeded.

When a Notice of Disapproval is issued, the examiner must record the applicant's unsatisfactory performance in terms of the AREA OF OPERATION and specific TASK(s) not meeting the standard appropriate to the practical test conducted. The AREA(s) OF OPERATION/TASK(s) not tested and the number of practical test failures must also be recorded. If the applicant fails the practical test because of a special emphasis area, the Notice of Disapproval must indicate the associated TASK. For example, SECTION 1, VIII. AREA OF OPERATION: SLOW FLIGHT AND STALLS, TASK A: MANEUVERING DURING SLOW FLIGHT, failure to use proper collision avoidance procedures.

Proficiency Check—Sport Pilot—Satisfactory Performance When Adding an Additional Category/Class

Satisfactory performance of TASKs to add category/class privileges is based on the applicant's ability to safely:

1. perform the TASKs specified in the AREAS OF OPERATION for the certificate or privileges sought within the approved standards;
2. demonstrate mastery of the aircraft with the successful outcome of each TASK performed never seriously in doubt;
3. demonstrate satisfactory proficiency and competency within the approved standards;
4. demonstrate sound judgment in aeronautical decision making/ risk management; and
5. demonstrate single-pilot competence.

When an applicant is adding a category/class privileges to his or her Sport Pilot Certificate, the authorized instructor, upon satisfactory completion of the proficiency check, must endorse the applicant's logbook indicating that the applicant is qualified to operate the additional sport pilot category/class of aircraft. The authorized instructor must forward FAA Form 8710-11 to Airman Registry within 10 days.

Proficiency Check—Sport Pilot—Unsatisfactory Performance When Adding an Additional Category/Class

When the applicant's performance does not meet the standards in the PTS, the authorized instructor conducting the proficiency check must annotate the unsatisfactory performance on the FAA Form 8710-11 and forward it to Airman Registry within 10 days. A Notice of Disapproval will **NOT** be issued in this instance; rather, the applicant should be provided with a list of the AREAS OF OPERATION and the specific TASKs not meeting the standard, so that the applicant may receive additional training.

When the applicant receives the additional training in the AREAS OF OPERATION and the specific TASK(s) found deficient during the proficiency check, the recommending instructor must endorse the applicant's logbook indicating that the applicant has received additional instruction and has been found competent to pass the proficiency check. The applicant must complete a new FAA Form 8710-11, and the recommending instructor must endorse the application. The authorized instructor, other than the one who provided the additional training, must evaluate the applicant. When the applicant successfully accomplishes a complete proficiency check, the authorized instructor, must forward the FAA Form 8710-11 to Airman Registry within 10 days and endorse the applicant's logbook indicating the airman's additional category/class privileges.

Single-Pilot Resource Management

Single-Pilot Resource Management refers to the effective use of ALL available resources: human resources, hardware, and information. It is similar to Crew Resource Management (CRM) procedures that are being emphasized in multi-crewmember operations except that only one crewmember (the pilot) is involved. Human resources "...includes all other groups routinely working with the pilot who are involved in decisions that are required to operate a flight safely. These groups include, but are not limited to: dispatchers, weather briefer, maintenance personnel, and air traffic controllers." Singe-pilot Resource Management is not a single TASK; it is a set of skill competencies that must be evident in all TASKs in this practical test standard as applied to single-pilot operation.

Applicant's Use of Checklists

Throughout the practical test or proficiency check, the applicant is evaluated on the use of an appropriate checklist (if specified by the manufacturer). Proper use is dependent on the specific TASK being evaluated. The situation may be such that the use of the checklist, while accomplishing elements of an Objective, would be either unsafe or impractical. In this case, a review of the checklist after the elements have been accomplished would be appropriate. Division of attention and proper visual scanning should be considered when using a checklist.

Use of Distractions During Practical Tests or Proficiency Checks

Numerous studies indicate that many accidents have occurred when the pilot has been distracted during critical phases of flight. To evaluate the applicant's ability to utilize proper control technique while dividing attention both inside and/or outside the cockpit, the examiner or authorized instructor must cause realistic distractions during the flight portion of the practical test or proficiency check to evaluate the applicant's ability to divide attention while maintaining safe flight.

Positive Exchange of Flight Controls

During flight, there must always be a clear understanding between the pilots of who has control of the aircraft. Prior to flight, a briefing should be conducted that includes the procedure for the exchange of flight controls. A positive three-step process in the exchange of flight controls between pilots is a proven procedure and one that is strongly recommended.

When one pilot wishes to give the other pilot control of the aircraft, he or she will say, "You have the flight controls." The pilot acknowledges immediately by saying, "I have the flight controls." The first pilot says again, "You have the flight controls." When control is returned to the first pilot, follow the same procedure. A visual check is recommended to verify that the exchange has occurred. There should never be any doubt as to who is flying the aircraft.

Letter of Discontinuance

When a practical test is discontinued for reasons other than unsatisfactory performance (i.e., equipment failure, weather, or illness), FAA Form 8710-11 and, if applicable, the Airman Knowledge Test Report must be returned to the applicant. The examiner at that time must prepare, sign, and issue a Letter of Discontinuance to the applicant. The Letter of Discontinuance should identify the AREAS OF OPERATION and their associated TASKs of the practical test that were successfully completed. The applicant must be advised that the Letter of Discontinuance must be presented to the examiner when the practical test is resumed, and made part of the certification file.

Aeronautical Decision Making and Risk Management

The examiner or authorized instructor must evaluate the applicant's ability throughout the practical test or proficiency check to use good aeronautical decision making procedures in order to evaluate risks. The examiner or authorized instructor must accomplish this requirement by developing scenarios that incorporate as many TASKs as possible to evaluate the applicants risk management in making safe aeronautical decisions. For example, the examiner or authorized instructor may develop a scenario that incorporates weather decisions and performance planning.

SECTION 1

SPORT PILOT

WEIGHT SHIFT CONTROL

(WSCL and WSCS)

SECTION 1—CONTENTS

SPORT PILOT WEIGHT SHIFT CONTROL

CHECKLISTS

AREAS OF OPERATION

APPLICANT'S PRACTICAL TEST CHECKLIST

APPOINTMENT WITH EXAMINER:

EXAMINER'S NAME_____

LOCATION _____

DATE/TIME _____

ACCEPTABLE AIRCRAFT

- ☐ Aircraft Documents: Airworthiness Certificate, Registration Certificate, and Operating Limitations
- ☐ Aircraft Maintenance Records: Logbook Record of Airworthiness Inspections/Safety Directives
- ☐ Pilot's Operating Handbook or FAA-Approved Flight Manual or Manufacturer's Operating Instructions

PERSONAL EQUIPMENT

- ☐ Current Aeronautical Charts
- ☐ Flight Logs
- ☐ Current AFD and Appropriate Publications

PERSONAL RECORDS

- ☐ Identification—Photo/Signature ID
- ☐ Pilot Certificate
- ☐ Medical Certificate or Driver's License
- ☐ Completed FAA Form 8710-11, Application for an Airman Certificate and/or Rating—Sport Pilot
- ☐ Airman Knowledge Test Report
- ☐ Logbook with Instructor's Endorsement
- ☐ FAA Form 8060-5, Notice of Disapproval (if applicable)
- ☐ Examiner's Fee (if applicable)

EXAMINER'S PRACTICAL TEST CHECKLIST

APPLICANT'S NAME _____

LOCATION _____

DATE/TIME _____

AREAS OF OPERATION

I. PREFLIGHT PREPARATION

- ☐ A. Certificates and Documents (WSCL and WSCS)
- ☐ B. Airworthiness Requirements (WSCL and WSCS)
- ☐ C. Weather Information (WSCL and WSCS)
- ☐ D. Cross-Country Flight Planning (WSCL and WSCS)
- ☐ E. National Airspace System (WSCL and WSCS)
- ☐ F. Operation of Systems (WSCL and WSCS)
- ☐ G. Aeromedical Factors (WSCL and WSCS)
- ☐ H. Water and Seaplane Characteristics (WSCS)
- ☐ I. Seaplane Bases, Maritime Rules, and Aids to Marine Navigation (WSCS)
- ☐ J. Performance and Limitations (WSCL and WSCS)
- ☐ K. Principles of Flight (WSCL and WSCS)

II. PREFLIGHT PROCEDURES

- ☐ A. Assembly (WSCL and WSCS)
- ☐ B. Wing Tuning (WSCL and WSCS)
- ☐ C. Preflight Inspection (WSCL and WSCS)
- ☐ D. Cockpit Management (WSCL and WSCS)
- ☐ E. Engine Starting (WSCL and WSCS)
- ☐ F. Taxiing (WSCL)
- ☐ G. Taxiing and Sailing (WSCS)
- ☐ H. Before Takeoff Check (WSCL and WSCS)

III. AIRPORT AND SEAPLANE BASE OPERATIONS

- ☐ A. Radio Communications (WSCL and WSCS)
- ☐ B. Traffic Patterns (WSCL and WSCS)
- ☐ C. Airport Runway Markings and Lighting (WSCL and WSCS)

IV. TAKEOFFS, LANDINGS, AND GO-AROUNDS

☐ A. Normal and Crosswind Takeoff and Climb (WSCL and WSCS)
☐ B. Power-on and Crosswind Approach and Landing (WSCL and WSCS)
☐ C. Glassy Water Takeoff and Climb (WSCS)
☐ D. Glassy Water Approach and Landing (WSCS)
☐ E. Rough Water Takeoff and Climb (WSCS)
☐ F. Rough Water Approach and Landing (WSCS)
☐ G. Steep Approach to a Landing (WSCL and WSCS)
☐ H. Go-around/Rejected Landing (WSCL and WSCS)

V. PERFORMANCE MANEUVER

☐ A. Steep Turns (WSCL and WSCS)

VI. GROUND REFERENCE MANEUVERS

☐ A. Rectangular Course (WSCL and WSCS)
☐ B. S-Turns (WSCL and WSCS)
☐ C. Turns Around a Point (WSCL and WSCS)

VII. NAVIGATION

☐ A. Pilotage and Dead Reckoning
☐ B. Diversion
☐ C. Lost Procedures

VIII. SLOW FLIGHT AND STALL

☐ A. Maneuvering During Slow Flight (WSCL and WSCS)
☐ B. Power-off Stall (WSCL and WSCS)
☐ C. Whip Stall and Tumble Awareness (WSCL and WSCS)

IX. EMERGENCY OPERATIONS

☐ A. Emergency Approach and Landing (Simulated) (WSCL and WSCS)
☐ B. Systems and Equipment Malfunctions (WSCL and WSCS)
☐ C. Emergency Equipment and Survival Gear (WSCL and WSCS)

X. POSTFLIGHT PROCEDURES

- ☐ A. After Landing, Parking, and Securing (WSCL and WSCS)
- ☐ B. Anchoring (WSCS)
- ☐ C. Docking and Mooring (WSCS)
- ☐ D. Ramping/Beaching (WSCS)

I. AREA OF OPERATION: PREFLIGHT PREPARATION

A. TASK: CERTIFICATES AND DOCUMENTS (WSCL and WSCS)

REFERENCES: 14 CFR parts 43, 61, 67, 91; FAA-H-8083-3, FAA-H-8083-25; Aircraft Flight Manual/POH/FAA Operating Limitations.

Objective. To determine that the applicant exhibits knowledge of the elements related to certificates and documents by:

1. Explaining—

    a. certificate privileges, limitations, and currency experience requirements.
    b. medical eligibility
    c. pilot logbook or flight records.

2. Locating and explaining—

    a. airworthiness and registration certificates.
    b. operating limitations, placards, instrument markings, Aircraft Flight Manual/POH, and flight training supplement.
    c. weight and balance data and/or equipment list, as applicable.

B. TASK: AIRWORTHINESS REQUIREMENTS (WSCL and WSCS)

REFERENCES: 14 CFR part 91; FAA-H-8083-25; Aircraft Operating Limitations.

Objective. To determine that the applicant exhibits knowledge of the elements related to airworthiness requirements by:

1. Explaining—

    a. required instruments and equipment for sport pilot privileges (as required by the operating limitations).
    b. procedures and limitations for determining if an aircraft, with inoperative instruments and or equipment, is airworthy or in a condition for safe operation.

2. Explaining—

    a. safety directives (as applicable to the aircraft brought for flight test).
    b. maintenance/inspection requirements and appropriate record keeping.

C. TASK: WEATHER INFORMATION (WSCL and WSCS)

REFERENCES: 14 CFR part 91; AC 00-6, AC 00-45, AC 61-84, AC 61-134; FAA-H-8083-3, FAA-H-8083-25; AIM.

Objective.   To determine that the applicant:

1. Exhibits knowledge of the elements related to real time weather information appropriate to the specific category/class aircraft by consulting weather reports, charts, and forecasts from aeronautical weather reporting sources.
2. Makes a competent "go/no-go" decision based on available weather information.
3. Describes the importance of avoiding adverse weather and inadvertent entry into instrument meteorological conditions (IMC).
4. Explains courses of action to safely exit from an inadvertent IMC encounter.

D. TASK: CROSS-COUNTRY FLIGHT PLANNING (WSCL and WSCS)

REFERENCES: 14 CFR part 91; FAA-H-8083-25; AC 61-84; Navigation Charts; A/FD; AIM.

Objective.   To determine that the applicant:

1. Exhibits knowledge of the elements related to cross-country flight planning appropriate to the category/class aircraft.
2. Uses appropriate and current aeronautical charts.
3. Properly identifies airspace, obstructions, and terrain features.
4. Selects easily identifiable en route checkpoints, as appropriate.
5. Selects most favorable altitudes considering weather conditions and equipment capabilities.
6. Determines headings, flight time, and fuel requirements.
7. Selects appropriate navigation system/facilities and communication frequencies, if so equipped.
8. Applies pertinent information from NOTAMs, AFD, and other flight publications.
9. Completes a navigation log and simulates filing a VFR flight plan.

E. TASK: NATIONAL AIRSPACE SYSTEM (WSCL and WSCS)

REFERENCES: 14 CFR parts 71, 91; Navigation Charts; AIM.

Objective.   To determine that the applicant exhibits knowledge of the elements related to the National Airspace System by explaining:

1. Sport pilot privileges applicable to the following classes of airspace—

    a.   Class B.
    b.   Class C.
    c.   Class D.
    d.   Class E.
    e.   Class G.

2. Special use and other airspace areas.
3. Temporary flight restrictions (TFRs).

F. TASK: OPERATION OF SYSTEMS (WSCL and WSCS)

REFERENCES: FAA-H-8083-25; Aircraft Flight Manual/POH.

Objective.   To determine that the applicant exhibits knowledge of the elements related to the operation of systems on the light-sport aircraft provided for the flight test by explaining at least three (3) of the following systems, if applicable:

1. Wing control and trim.
2. Water rudders, if applicable.
3. Powerplant and propeller, if applicable.
4. Landing gear.
5. Fuel, oil, hydraulic, and coolant system (if liquid cooled).
6. Electrical.
7. Avionics and auxiliary equipment (if installed).
8. Pitot-static, vacuum/pressure, and associated flight instruments, as appropriate.

G. TASK: AEROMEDICAL FACTORS (WSCL and WSCS)

REFERENCES: FAA-H-8083-25; AIM.

Objective. To determine that the applicant exhibits knowledge of the elements related to aeromedical factors by explaining:

1. The effects of alcohol, drugs and over-the-counter medications.
2. The symptoms, causes, effects, and corrective actions of at least three (3) of the following—

   a. hypoxia.
   b. hyperventilation.
   c. middle ear and sinus problems.
   d. spatial disorientation.
   e. motion sickness.
   f. carbon monoxide poisoning.
   g. stress and fatigue.
   h. dehydration.
   i. hypothermia.

H. TASK: WATER AND SEAPLANE CHARACTERISTICS (WSCS)

REFERENCE: FAA-H-8083-23.

Objective. To determine that the applicant exhibits knowledge of the elements related to water and seaplane characteristics by explaining:

1. The characteristics of a water surface as affected by features, such as—

   a. size and location.
   b. protected and unprotected areas.
   c. surface wind.
   d. direction and strength of water current.
   e. floating and partially submerged debris.
   f. sandbars, islands, and shoals.
   g. vessel traffic and wakes.
   h. other features peculiar to the area.

2. Float and hull construction, and their effect on seaplane performance.
3. Causes of porpoising and skipping, and the pilot action required to prevent or correct these occurrences.

I. **TASK:** **SEAPLANE BASES, MARITIME RULES, AND AIDS TO MARINE NAVIGATION (WSCS)**

REFERENCES: FAA-H-8083-23; AIM.

Objective. To determine that the applicant exhibits knowledge of the elements related to seaplane bases, maritime rules, and aids to marine navigation by explaining:

1. How to locate and identify seaplane bases on charts or in directories.
2. Operating restrictions at seaplane bases, if applicable.
3. Right-of-way, steering, and sailing rules pertinent to seaplane operation.
4. Marine navigation aids such as buoys, beacons, lights, and sound signals.

J. **TASK:** **PERFORMANCE AND LIMITATIONS (WSCL and WSCS)**

REFERENCES: FAA-H-8083-1, FAA-H-8083-23, FAA-H-8083-25; Aircraft Flight Manual/POH.

Objective. To determine the applicant:

1. Exhibits knowledge of the elements related to performance and limitations by explaining the use of charts, tables, and data if appropriate, to determine performance and the adverse effects of exceeding limitations.
2. Exhibits knowledge of the center of gravity on weight shift performance.
3. Describes the effects of atmospheric conditions on the weight shift's performance.
4. Explains the effects and hazards of high wind, referencing the ground speed, high rates of turn and power requirements on making downwind turns in close proximity to the ground.

K. TASK: PRINCIPLES OF FLIGHT (WSCL and WSCS)

REFERENCES: FAA-H-8083-25; Aircraft Flight Manual/POH.

Objective. To determine the applicant exhibits knowledge of basic aerodynamics and principles of flight including:

1. Forces acting on a weight shift machine in various flight maneuvers.
2. Weight shift stability and controllability.
3. Loads and load factors.
4. Angle of attack, stalls and stall recovery, including flight situations in which unintentional stalls may occur.
5. Effects and use of wing control, including the purpose and proper technique for use.

II. AREA OF OPERATION: PREFLIGHT PROCEDURES

NOTE: **For single-seat applicants,** the examiner shall select at least TASKs A, B, C, E, and one other TASK as applicable.

A. TASK: ASSEMBLY (WSCL AND WSCS)

NOTE: If, in the judgment of the examiner, the demonstration of the WSC assembly is impractical, competency may be determined by oral testing.

REFERENCES: Aircraft Flight Manual/POH.

Objective. To determine that the applicant:

1. Exhibits knowledge of the elements related to the assembly procedures following the manufacturer's procedures.
2. Selects a suitable assembly area and provides sufficient crewmembers for assembly.
3. Follows the appropriate checklist.
4. Uses proper tools.
5. Handles components properly.
6. Cleans and lubricates parts, as appropriate.
7. Accounts for all tools and parts at the completion of assembly.
8. Performs post-assembly inspections, including a control check.

B. TASK: WING TUNING (WSCL and WSCS)

REFERENCES: Aircraft Flight Manual/POH.

Objective. To determine that the applicant:

1. Exhibits knowledge of the elements related to wing tuning procedures.
2. Describes the correct procedures for tuning the wing to fly straight.
3. Describes the correct procedures for tuning the wing to fly faster or slower.
4. Exhibits knowledge of the relationship between speed and stability with regard to wing tuning.

C. TASK: PREFLIGHT INSPECTION (WSCL and WSCS)

REFERENCES: AC 61-84; Aircraft Flight Manual/POH.

Objective. To determine that the applicant:

1. Exhibits knowledge of the elements related to preflight inspection. This shall include which items must be inspected, the reasons for checking each item, and how to detect possible defects.
2. Inspects the weight shift control aircraft with reference to an appropriate checklist.
3. Verifies the weight shift control aircraft is in condition for safe flight.

D. TASK: COCKPIT MANAGEMENT (WSCL and WSCS)

REFERENCES: FAA-H-8083-25; Aircraft Flight Manual/POH.

Objective. To determine that the applicant:

1. Exhibits knowledge of the elements related to cockpit management procedures.
2. Ensures all loose items in the cockpit and on each occupant are removed, stowed, or secured.
3. Organizes material and equipment in an efficient manner so they are readily available.
4. Briefs occupant on the use of safety belts, shoulder harnesses, doors, and emergency procedures.

E. TASK: ENGINE STARTING (WSCL and WSCS)

REFERENCES: FAA-H-8083-25; Aircraft Flight Manual/POH.

Objective. To determine that the applicant:

1. Exhibits knowledge of the elements related to recommended engine starting procedures.
2. Positions the weight shift control aircraft properly considering structures, surface conditions, other aircraft, and the safety of nearby persons and property.

F. TASK: TAXIING (WSCL)

REFERENCES: FAA-H-8083-25; Aircraft Flight Manual/POH.

Objective. To determine that the applicant:

1. Exhibits knowledge of the elements related to safe taxi procedures.
2. Performs a brake check immediately after the weight shift control aircraft begins moving.
3. Positions the wing properly for the existing wind conditions.
4. Controls direction and speed without excessive use of brakes.
5. Complies with airport/taxiway markings, signals, ATC clearances, and instructions.
6. Taxies so as to avoid other aircraft and hazards.

G. TASK: TAXIING AND SAILING (WSCS)

REFERENCES: FAA-H-8083-23; USCG Navigation Rules; International-Inland; Aircraft Flight Manual/POH.

Objective. To determine that the applicant:

1. Exhibits knowledge of the elements related to water taxiing and sailing procedures.
2. Positions the wing properly for the existing wind conditions.
3. Plans and follows the most favorable course while taxi or sailing considering wind, water current, water conditions and maritime regulations.
4. Uses the appropriate idle, plow, or step taxi technique.
5. Uses wing, water rudder, and power correctly so as to follow the desired course while sailing.
6. Prevents and corrects for porpoising and skipping.
7. Avoids other aircraft, vessels, and hazards.
8. Complies with seaplane base signs, signals, and clearances.

H. TASK: BEFORE TAKEOFF CHECK (WSCL and WSCS)

REFERENCES: FAA-H-8083-3, FAA-H-8083-23; Aircraft Flight Manual/POH.

Objective. To determine that the applicant:

1. Exhibits knowledge of the elements related to the before takeoff check. This shall include the reasons for checking each item and how to detect malfunctions.
2. Positions the weight shift control aircraft properly considering other aircraft/vessels, wind and surface conditions.
3. Divides attention inside and outside the cockpit.
4. Ensures that engine temperature is suitable for takeoff.
5. Accomplishes the before takeoff checklist and ensures the weight shift control aircraft is in safe operating condition.
6. Reviews takeoff performance airspeeds, takeoff distances, departure, and emergency procedures.
7. Avoids runway incursions and/or ensures no conflict with traffic prior to taxiing into takeoff position.
8. Completes the appropriate checklist.

III. AREA OF OPERATION: AIRPORT AND SEAPLANE BASE OPERATIONS

A. TASK: RADIO COMMUNICATIONS (WSCL and WSCS)

NOTE: If the aircraft is not radio equipped, this TASK shall be tested orally for procedures ONLY.

REFERENCES: 14 CFR part 91; FAA-H-8083-25; AIM.

Objective. To determine that the applicant:

1. Exhibits knowledge of the elements related to radio communications at airports without operating control towers.
2. Selects appropriate frequencies.
3. Transmits using recommended phraseology.
4. Acknowledges radio communications.

B. TASK: TRAFFIC PATTERNS (WSCL and WSCS)

REFERENCES: FAA-H-8083-3, FAA-H-8083-25; AC 90-66; AIM.

Objective. To determine that the applicant:

1. Exhibits knowledge of the elements related to traffic patterns at airports without operating control towers, prevention of runway incursions, collision avoidance, wake turbulence avoidance, and wind shear.
2. Complies with proper local traffic pattern procedures.
3. Maintains proper spacing from other aircraft.
4. Corrects for wind drift to maintain the proper ground track.
5. Maintains orientation with the runway/landing area in use.
6. Maintains traffic pattern altitude, ±100 feet, and the appropriate airspeed, ±10 knots, if applicable.

C. TASK: AIRPORT RUNWAY MARKINGS AND LIGHTING (WSCL and WSCS)

REFERENCES: FAA-H-8083-23, FAA-H-8083-25; AIM.

Objective.   To determine that the applicant:

1. Exhibits knowledge of the elements related to airport/seaplane base, markings and lighting with emphasis on runway incursion avoidance.
2. Properly identifies and interprets airport/seaplane base markings and lighting.

IV. AREA OF OPERATION: TAKEOFFS, LANDINGS, AND GO-AROUNDS

NOTE: For single-seat applicants, the examiner shall select all TASKs.

A. TASK: NORMAL AND CROSSWIND TAKEOFF AND CLIMB (WSCL and WSCS)

NOTE: If a crosswind condition does not exist, the applicant's knowledge of crosswind elements shall be evaluated through oral testing.

REFERENCES: FAA-H-8083-3, FAA-H-8083-23; POH/AFM.

Objective. To determine that the applicant:

1. Exhibits knowledge of the elements related to normal crosswind takeoff and climb, including rejected takeoff procedures.
2. Positions the wing for the existing wind conditions.
3. Clears the area; taxies into the takeoff position and aligns the weight shift control aircraft on the runway center/takeoff path.
4. Advances the throttle smoothly to takeoff power. (WSCS)
5. Establishes and maintains the most efficient planing/lift off attitude and corrects for porpoising and skipping. (WSCS)
6. Lifts off at the recommended airspeed and accelerates to appropriate climb speed.
7. Establishes a pitch attitude that will maintain appropriate climb speed +10/−5 knots or speed recommended by the Aircraft Flight Manual/POH to maintain control if you have an engine failure.
8. Maintains takeoff power to a safe maneuvering altitude.
9. Maintains directional control and proper wind-drift correction throughout the takeoff and climb.

B. TASK: POWER-ON AND CROSSWIND APPROACH AND LANDING (WSCL and WSCS)

NOTE: If a crosswind condition does not exist, the applicant's knowledge of crosswind elements shall be evaluated through oral testing.

REFERENCES: FAA-H-8083-3, FAA-H-8083-23; Aircraft Flight Manual/POH.

Objective. To determine that the applicant:

1. Exhibits knowledge of the elements related to a power-on and crosswind approach and landing.
2. Adequately surveys the intended landing area. (WSCS)
3. Considers the wind conditions, landing surface, obstructions, and selects a suitable touchdown point.
4. Establishes the recommended approach and landing configuration (water rudders down) and airspeed, and adjusts pitch attitude and power as required.
5. Maintains a stabilized approach and recommended airspeed.
6. Makes smooth, timely, and correct control application during the roundout and touchdown.
7. Contacts the water at the proper pitch attitude. (WSCS)
8. Touches down smoothly at appropriate airspeed. (WSCL)
9. Touches down at or within 400 feet beyond a specified point, with no drift, and with the weight shift control aircraft's flight path aligned with and over the runway center/landing path.
10. Maintains directional control throughout the approach and landing sequence.

C. TASK: GLASSY WATER TAKEOFF AND CLIMB (WSCS)

NOTE: If glassy water condition does not exist, the applicant shall be evaluated by simulating the TASK.

REFERENCES: FAA-H-8083-23; Aircraft Flight Manual/POH.

Objective. To determine that the applicant:

1. Exhibits knowledge of the elements related to glassy water takeoff and climb.
2. Positions the wing for the existing conditions.
3. Clears the area; selects an appropriate takeoff path considering surface hazards and/or vessels and surface conditions.
4. Advances the throttle smoothly to takeoff power.
5. Establishes and maintains an appropriate planing attitude, directional control, and corrects for porpoising, skipping, and increases in water drag.
6. Utilizes appropriate techniques to lift aircraft from the water considering surface conditions.
7. Establishes proper attitude/airspeed, and accelerates to best climb or speed recommended by the Aircraft Flight Manual/POH +10/−5 knots during the climb.
8. Maintains takeoff power to a safe maneuvering altitude.
9. Maintains directional control and proper wind-drift correction throughout takeoff and climb.

D. TASK: GLASSY WATER APPROACH AND LANDING (WSCS)

NOTE: If glassy water condition does not exist, the applicant shall be evaluated by simulating the TASK.

REFERENCES: FAA-H-8083-23; Aircraft Flight Manual/POH.

Objective.   To determine that the applicant:

1. Exhibits knowledge of the elements related to glassy water approach and landing.
2. Adequately surveys the intended landing area.
3. Considers the wind conditions, water depth, hazards, surrounding terrain, and other watercraft.
4. Selects the most suitable approach path, and touchdown area.
5. Establishes the recommended approach and landing configuration (water rudders down) and airspeed, and adjusts pitch attitude and power as required.
6. Maintains a stabilized approach and the recommended approach airspeed, or speed recommended by the Aircraft Flight Manual/POH, +10/−5 knots and maintains a touchdown pitch attitude and descent rate from the last altitude reference until touchdown.
7. Makes smooth, timely, and correct power and control adjustments to maintain proper pitch attitude and rate of descent to touchdown.
8. Contacts the water in the proper pitch attitude, and slows to idle taxi speed.
9. Maintains directional control throughout the approach and landing sequence.

E. TASK: ROUGH WATER TAKEOFF AND CLIMB (WSCS)

NOTE: If rough water condition does not exist, the applicant shall be evaluated by simulating the TASK.

REFERENCES: FAA-H-8083-23; Aircraft Flight Manual/POH.

Objective. To determine that the applicant:

1. Exhibits knowledge of the elements related to rough water takeoff and climb.
2. Positions the wing for the existing conditions.
3. Clears the area; selects an appropriate takeoff path considering wind, swells surface hazards and/or vessels.
4. Establishes and maintains an appropriate planing attitude, directional control, and corrects for porpoising, skipping, or excessive bouncing.
5. Lifts off at minimum airspeed and accelerates to best climb or speed recommended by the Aircraft Flight Manual/POH, +10/−5 knots before leaving ground effect.
6. Maintains takeoff power to a safe maneuvering altitude.
7. Maintains directional control and proper wind-drift correction throughout takeoff and climb.

F. TASK: ROUGH WATER APPROACH AND LANDING (WSCS)

NOTE: If rough water condition does not exist, the applicant shall be evaluated by simulating the TASK.

REFERENCES: FAA-H-8083-23; Aircraft Flight Manual/POH.

Objective. To determine that the applicant:

1. Exhibits knowledge of the elements related to rough water approach and landing.
2. Adequately surveys the intended landing area.
3. Considers the wind conditions, water, depth, hazards, surrounding terrain, and other watercraft.
4. Selects the most suitable approach path, and touchdown area.
5. Establishes the recommended approach and landing configuration (water rudders down) and airspeed, and adjusts pitch attitude and power as required.
6. Maintains a stabilized approach and the recommended approach airspeed, +10/−5 knots with wind gust factor applied.
7. Makes smooth, timely, and correct power and control application during the roundout and touch down.
8. Contacts the water in the proper pitch attitude, and at the proper airspeed, considering the type of rough water.
9. Maintains directional control throughout the approach and landing sequence.

G. TASK: STEEP APPROACH TO A LANDING (WSCL and WSCS)

REFERENCES: FAA-H-8083-3; Aircraft Flight Manual/POH.

Objective. To determine that the applicant:

1. Exhibits knowledge of the elements related to a steep approach to a landing.
2. Adequately surveys the intended landing area. (WSCS)
3. Considers the wind conditions, landing surface and obstructions, and selects a suitable touchdown point.
4. Demonstrates effective use of controls at the point from which a landing can be made using steep approach techniques.
5. Establishes a ground track aligned with the runway centerline and an airspeed, which results in minimum float during the roundout.
6. Makes smooth, timely, and correct control application during the recovery from the maneuvers, the roundout, and the touchdown.
7. Contacts the water at the proper pitch attitude. (WSCS)
8. Touches down smoothly at appropriate airspeed. (WSCS)
9. Touches down smoothly at an appropriate speed, at or within 400 feet beyond a specified point, with no side drift, and with the weight shift aircraft's ground track aligned with and over the runway centerline.
10. Maintains directional control throughout the approach and landing.

H. TASK: GO-AROUND/REJECTED LANDING (WSCL and WSCS)

REFERENCES: FAA-H-8083-3; Aircraft Flight Manual/POH.

Objective. To determine that the applicant:

1. Exhibits knowledge of the elements related to a go-around/rejected landing.
2. Makes a timely decision to discontinue the approach to landing.
3. Applies takeoff power immediately and transitions to climb pitch attitude for best climb and maintains appropriate climb or speed recommended by the Aircraft Flight Manual/POH +10/−5 knots.
4. Maneuvers to the side of the runway/landing area to clear and avoid conflicting traffic.
5. Maintains takeoff power to a safe maneuvering altitude.
6. Maintains directional control and proper wind-drift correction throughout the climb.

V. AREA OF OPERATION: PERFORMANCE MANEUVERS

A. TASK: STEEP TURNS (WSCL and WSCS)

REFERENCES: FAA-H-8083-3; Aircraft Flight Manual/POH.

Objective.   To determine that the applicant:

1. Exhibits knowledge of the elements related to steep turns.
2. Establishes the manufacturers recommended airspeed.
3. Rolls into a 360° turn; maintains a 45° bank.
4. Performs the task in opposite direction, as specified by the examiner.
5. Divides attention between aircraft control and orientation.
6. Maintains the entry altitude ±100 feet, airspeed ±10 knots, bank ±10°, and rolls out on the entry heading ±10°.

VI. AREA OF OPERATION: GROUND REFERENCE MANEUVERS

NOTE: The examiner shall select at least one TASK.

NOTE: For single-seat applicants, the examiner shall select TASK A.

A. TASK: RECTANGULAR COURSE (WSCL and WSCS)

REFERENCE: FAA-H-8083-3.

Objective.   To determine that the applicant:

1. Exhibits knowledge of the elements related to a rectangular course.
2. Selects a suitable reference area.
3. Plans the maneuver so as to not descend below 400 feet above the ground at an appropriate distance from the selected reference area, 45° to the downwind leg.
4. Applies adequate wind-drift correction during straight-and-turning flight to maintain a constant ground track around the rectangular reference area.
5. Divides attention between aircraft control and the ground track.
6. Maintains altitude, ±100 feet; maintains airspeed, ±10 knots.

B. TASK: S-TURNS (WSCL and WSCS)

REFERENCE: FAA-H-8083-3.

Objective.   To determine that the applicant:

1. Exhibits knowledge of the elements related to S-turns.
2. Selects a suitable ground reference line.
3. Plans the maneuver so as to not descend below 400 feet above the ground perpendicular to the selected reference line.
4. Applies adequate wind-drift correction to track a constant radius turn on each side of the selected reference line.
5. Reverses the direction of turn directly over the selected reference line.
6. Divides attention between aircraft control and the ground track.
7. Maintains altitude, ±100 feet; maintains airspeed, ±10 knots.

C. TASK: TURNS AROUND A POINT (WSCL and WSCS)

REFERENCE: FAA-H-8083-3.

Objective.   To determine that the applicant:

1. Exhibits knowledge of the elements related to turns around a point.
2. Selects a suitable ground reference point.
3. Plans the maneuver so as to not descend below 400 feet above the ground, at an appropriate distance from the reference point.
4. Applies adequate wind-drift correction to track a constant radius turn around the selected reference point.
5. Divides attention between aircraft control and the ground track.
6. Maintains altitude, ±100 feet; maintains airspeed, ±10 knots.

VII. AREA OF OPERATION: NAVIGATION

A. TASK: PILOTAGE AND DEAD RECKONING

REFERENCE: FAA-H-8083-25.

Objective. To determine that the applicant:

1. Exhibits knowledge of the elements related to pilotage and dead reckoning, as appropriate.
2. Follows the preplanned course by reference to landmarks.
3. Identifies landmarks by relating surface features to chart symbols.
4. Verifies the aircraft's position within 3 nautical miles of the flight-planned route.
5. Determines there is sufficient fuel to complete the planned flight, if not, has an alternate plan.
6. Maintains the appropriate altitude, ±200 feet, and headings, ±15°.

B. TASK: DIVERSION

REFERENCES: FAA-8083-25; AIM.

Objective. To determine that the applicant:

1. Exhibits knowledge of the elements related to diversion.
2. Selects an appropriate alternate airport or landing area and route.
3. Determines there is sufficient fuel to fly to the alternate airport or landing area.
4. Turns to and establishes a course to the selected alternate destination.
5. Maintains the appropriate altitude, ±200 feet, and headings, ±15°.

C. TASK: LOST PROCEDURES

REFERENCES: FAA-H-8083-25; AIM.

Objective. To determine that the applicant:

1. Exhibits knowledge of the elements related to lost procedures.
2. Selects an appropriate course of action.
3. Maintains an appropriate heading and climbs if necessary.
4. Identifies prominent landmarks.
5. Uses navigation systems/facilities and or contacts an ATC facility for assistance, as appropriate.

VIII. AREA OF OPERATION: SLOW FLIGHT AND STALLS

A. TASK: MANEUVERING DURING SLOW FLIGHT (WSCL and WSCS)

REFERENCES: FAA-H-8083-3, Aircraft Flight Manual/POH.

Objective. To determine that the applicant:

1. Exhibits knowledge of the elements related to maneuvering during slow flight.
2. Selects an entry altitude that will allow the task to be completed no lower than 1,000 feet AGL.
3. Establishes and maintains a minimum flying airspeed.
4. Accomplishes straight-and-level flight, turns, climbs, and descents specified by the examiner.
5. Divides attention between weight shift control aircraft control and orientation.
6. Maintains the specified altitude, ±100 feet; specified heading, ±10°; airspeed, +10/−5 knots, and specified angle of bank, ±10°.

B. TASK: POWER-OFF STALL (WSCL and WSCS)

REFERENCES: AC 61-67; FAA-H-8083-3; Aircraft Flight Manual/POH.

Objective. To determine that the applicant:

1. Exhibits knowledge of the elements related to power-off stalls.
2. Selects an entry altitude that allows the task to be completed no lower than 1,000 feet AGL.
3. Establishes a stabilized descent in the approach or landing configuration, as specified by the examiner. Transitions smoothly from the approach or landing attitude to a pitch attitude that will induce a stall.
4. Maintains a specified heading, ±10°, in straight flight; maintains a specified angle of bank not to exceed 20°, ±10°; in turning flight, while inducing the stall.
5. Recognizes and recovers promptly after the stall occurs by simultaneously reducing the angle of attack, increasing power to maximum allowable, and leveling the wing to return to a straight-and-level flight attitude with a minimum loss of altitude appropriate for the weight shift control aircraft.
6. Accelerates to normal speed; returns to the altitude, heading, and airspeed specified by the examiner.

C. TASK: WHIP STALL AND TUMBLE AWARENESS (WSCL and WSCS)

NOTE: The applicant's knowledge of whipstall and tumble awareness shall be evaluated through oral testing only.

REFERENCES: AC 61-67; FAA-H-8083-3; Aircraft Flight Manual/POH.

Objective.   To determine that the applicant exhibits knowledge of the elements related to whip stall and tumble awareness by explaining:

  1.   Elements related to whip stalls and tumbles.
  2.   Flight situations where unintentional whip stalls and tumbles may occur.
  3.   The techniques used to avoid whipstalls and tumbles.
  4.   The likely results of executing a whip stall or tumble.

IX. AREA OF OPERATION: EMERGENCY OPERATIONS

NOTE: For single-seat applicants, the examiner shall select TASK A.

A. TASK: EMERGENCY APPROACH AND LANDING (SIMULATED) (WSCL and WSCS)

REFERENCES: FAA-H-8083-3; Aircraft Flight Manual/POH.

Objective. To determine that the applicant:

1. Exhibits knowledge of the elements related to emergency approach and landing procedures, including energy management.
2. Establishes and maintains the recommended best glide and airspeed, ±10 knots.
3. Selects a suitable landing area.
4. Plans and follows a flight pattern to the selected landing area considering altitude, wind, terrain, and obstructions.
5. Prepares for landing, or go-around, as specified by the examiner.

B. TASK: SYSTEMS AND EQUIPMENT MALFUNCTIONS (WSCL and WSCS)

REFERENCES: FAA-H-8083-25; Aircraft Flight Manual/POH.

Objective. To determine that the applicant:

1. Exhibits knowledge of the elements related to system and equipment malfunctions appropriate to the weight shift control aircraft provided for the practical test.
2. Analyzes the situation and takes appropriate action for simulated emergencies appropriate to the weight shift control aircraft provided for the practical test for at least three (3) of the following—

    a. partial or complete power loss.
    b. engine roughness or overheat.
    c. carburetor or induction icing.
    d. loss of oil pressure.
    e. fuel starvation.
    f. electrical malfunction.
    g. flight instruments malfunction.
    h. pitot/static.
    i. landing gear malfunction.
    j. smoke/fire/engine compartment fire.
    k. inadvertent prop strike.
    l. ballistic recovery system if applicable.
    m. any other emergency appropriate to the weight shift aircraft.

3. Follows the appropriate procedure.

C. TASK: EMERGENCY EQUIPMENT AND SURVIVAL GEAR (WSCL and WSCS)

REFERENCES: AC 91-13, AC 91-58, AC 91-69; Aircraft Flight Manual/POH.

Objective. To determine that the applicant exhibits knowledge of the elements related to emergency equipment appropriate to the following environmental conditions:

1. mountainous terrain.
2. large bodies of water.
3. desert conditions.
4. extreme temperature changes.

X. AREA OF OPERATION: POSTFLIGHT PROCEDURES

NOTE: The examiner shall select Task A and for ASES applicants at least one other TASK.

NOTE: For single-seat applicants, the examiner shall select TASK A and for WSCS applicants at least one other TASK.

A. TASK: AFTER LANDING, PARKING, AND SECURING (WSCL and WSCS)

REFERENCES: FAA-H-8083-3, FAA-H-8083-23; Aircraft Flight Manual/POH.

Objective. To determine that the applicant:

1. Exhibits knowledge of the elements related to after landing, parking and securing procedures.
2. Maintains directional control after touchdown while decelerating to an appropriate speed.
3. Observes runway hold lines and other surface control markings and lighting.
4. Parks in an appropriate area, considering the safety of nearby persons and property.
5. Follows the appropriate procedure for engine shutdown.
6. Conducts an appropriate postflight inspection and secures the aircraft wing while exiting the aircraft, and properly securing the aircraft in high wind conditions.
7. Completes the appropriate checklist.

B. TASK: ANCHORING (WSCS)

REFERENCES: FAA-H-8083-23; Aircraft Flight Manual/POH.

Objective. To determine that the applicant:

1. Exhibits knowledge of the elements related to anchoring.
2. Selects a suitable area for anchoring, considering aircraft movement, water depth, tide, wind, and weather changes.
3. Uses an adequate number of anchors and lines of sufficient strength and length to ensure the aircraft's security.

C. TASK: DOCKING AND MOORING (WSCS)

REFERENCES: FAA-H-8083-23; Aircraft Flight Manual/POH.

Objective.   To determine that the applicant:

1. Exhibits knowledge of the elements related to docking and mooring.
2. Approaches the dock or mooring buoy in the proper direction considering speed hazards, wind, and water current.
3. Ensures aircraft security.

D. TASK: RAMPING/BEACHING (WSCS)

REFERENCES: FAA-H-8083-23; Aircraft Flight Manual/POH.

Objective.   To determine that the applicant:

1. Exhibits knowledge of the elements related to ramping/beaching.
2. Approaches the ramp/beach considering persons and property, in the proper attitude and direction, at a safe speed, considering water depth, tide, current and wind.
3. Ramps/beaches and secures the aircraft in a manner that will protect it from the harmful effect of wind, waves, and changes in water level.

SECTION 2

SPORT PILOT

POWERED PARACHUTE

(PPCL and PPCS)

SECTION 2—CONTENTS

SPORT PILOT POWERED PARACHUTE

CHECKLISTS

AREAS OF OPERATION

IX. POSTFLIGHT PROCEDURES 2-22

APPLICANT'S PRACTICAL TEST CHECKLIST

APPOINTMENT WITH EXAMINER:

EXAMINER'S NAME_____

LOCATION _____

DATE/TIME _____

ACCEPTABLE AIRCRAFT

- ☐ Aircraft Documents: Airworthiness Certificate, Registration Certificate, and Operating Limitations
- ☐ Aircraft Maintenance Records: Logbook Record of Airworthiness Inspections/Safety Directives
- ☐ Pilot's Operating Handbook or FAA-Approved Flight Manual or Manufacturer's Operating Instructions

PERSONAL EQUIPMENT

- ☐ Current Aeronautical Chart
- ☐ Flight Logs
- ☐ Current AFD and Appropriate Publications

PERSONAL RECORDS

- ☐ Identification—Photo/Signature ID
- ☐ Pilot Certificate
- ☐ Medical Certificate or Driver's License
- ☐ Completed FAA Form 8710-11, Application for an Airman Certificate and/or Rating—Sport Pilot
- ☐ Airman Knowledge Test Report
- ☐ Logbook with Instructor's Endorsement
- ☐ FAA Form 8060-5, Notice of Disapproval (if applicable)
- ☐ Examiner's Fee (if applicable)

EXAMINER'S PRACTICAL TEST CHECKLIST

APPLICANT'S NAME_____

LOCATION_____

DATE/TIME_____

AREAS OF OPERATION

I. PREFLIGHT PREPARATION

- ☐ A. Certificates and Documents (PPCL and PPCS)
- ☐ B. Airworthiness Requirements (PPCL and PPCS)
- ☐ C. Weather Information (PPCL and PPCS)
- ☐ D. Cross-Country Flight Planning (PPCL and PPCS)
- ☐ E. National Airspace System (PPCL and PPCS)
- ☐ F. Operation of Systems (PPCL and PPCS)
- ☐ G. Aeromedical Factors (PPCL and PPCS)
- ☐ H. Water and Seaplane Characteristics (PPCS)
- ☐ I. Seaplane Bases, Maritime Rules, and Aids To Marine Navigation (PPCS)
- ☐ J. Performance and Limitations (PPCL and PPCS)
- ☐ K. Principles of Flight (PPCL and PPCS)

II. PREFLIGHT PROCEDURES

- ☐ A. Preflight Inspection (PPCL and PPCS)
- ☐ B. Canopy Layout (PPCL and PPCS)
- ☐ C. Engine Warm Up/Starting (PPCL and PPCS)
- ☐ D. Cockpit Management (PPCL and PPCS)
- ☐ E. Taxiing (Canopy Inflated) (PPCL and PPCS)
- ☐ F. Taxiing and Sailing (PPCS)
- ☐ G. Before Takeoff Check (PPCL and PPCS)

III. AIRPORT AND SEAPLANE BASE OPERATIONS

- ☐ A. Radio Communications (PPCL and PPCS)
- ☐ B. Traffic Patterns (PPCL and PPCS)
- ☐ C. Airport Runway Markings and Lighting (PPCL and PPCS)

IV. TAKEOFFS, LANDINGS, AND GO-AROUNDS

- ☐ A. Normal Takeoff and Climb (PPCL and PPCS)
- ☐ B. Normal Approach and Landing (PPCL and PPCS)
- ☐ C. Glassy Water Takeoff and Climb (PPCS)
- ☐ D. Glassy Water Approach and Landing (PPCS)
- ☐ E. Rough Water Takeoff and Climb (PPCS)
- ☐ F. Rough Water Approach and Landing (PPCS)
- ☐ G. Go-around/Rejected Landing (PPCL and PPCS)

V. PERFORMANCE MANEUVERS

- ☐ A. Constant Altitude Turns (PPCL and PPCS)

VI. GROUND REFERENCE MANEUVERS

- ☐ A. Rectangular Course (PPCL and PPCS)
- ☐ B. S-Turns (PPCL and PPCS)
- ☐ C. Turns Around a Point (PPCL and PPCS)

VII. NAVIGATION

- ☐ A. Pilotage and Dead Reckoning (PPCL and PPCS)
- ☐ B. Diversion (PPCL and PPCS)
- ☐ C. Lost Procedures (PPCL and PPCS)

VIII. EMERGENCY OPERATIONS

- ☐ A. Emergency Approach and Landing (Simulated) (PPCL and PPCS)
- ☐ B. Systems and Equipment Malfunctions (PPCL and PPCS)
- ☐ C. Emergency Equipment and Survival Gear (PPCL and .. PPCS)

IX. POSTFLIGHT PROCEDURES

- ☐ A. After Landing, Parking, and Securing (PPCL and PPCS)
- ☐ B. Anchoring (PPCS)
- ☐ C. Docking and Mooring (PPCS)
- ☐ D. Ramping/Beaching (PPCS)

I. AREA OF OPERATION: PREFLIGHT PREPARATION

A. TASK: CERTIFICATES AND DOCUMENTS (PPCL and PPCS)

REFERENCES: 14 CFR parts 43, 61, 67, 91; FAA-H-8083-3, FAA-H-8083-25, FAA-H-8083-29; Aircraft Flight Manual/POH/FAA Operating Limitations.

Objective. To determine that the applicant exhibits knowledge of the elements related to certificates and documents by:

1. Explaining—

   a. certificate privileges, limitations, and currency experience requirements.
   b. medical eligibility.
   c. pilot logbook or flight records.

2. Locating and explaining—

   a. airworthiness and registration certificates.
   b. operating limitations, placards, instrument markings, and flight training supplement.
   c. weight and balance data and/or equipment list, as applicable.

B. TASK: AIRWORTHINESS REQUIREMENTS (PPCL and PPCS)

REFERENCES: 14 CFR part 91; FAA-H-8083-25, FAA-H-8083-29; Aircraft Operating Limitations.

Objective. To determine that the applicant exhibits knowledge of the elements related to airworthiness requirements by:

1. Explaining—

   a. required instruments and equipment for sport pilot privileges (as required by the operating limitations).
   b. procedures and limitations for determining if the aircraft, with inoperative instruments and/or equipment, is airworthy or in a condition for safe operation.

2. Explaining—

   a. safety directives (as applicable to the aircraft brought for flight test).
   b. maintenance/inspection requirements and appropriate record keeping.

C. TASK: WEATHER INFORMATION (PPCL and PPCS)

REFERENCES: 14 CFR part 91; AC 00-6, AC 00-45, AC 61-84, AC 61-134; FAA-H-8083-3, FAA-H-8083-25, FAA-H-8083-29; AIM.

Objective. To determine that the applicant:

1. Exhibits knowledge of the elements related to real time weather information appropriate to the specific category/class aircraft by consulting weather reports, charts and forecasts from aeronautical weather reporting sources.
2. Makes a competent "go/no-go" decision based on available weather information.
3. Describes the importance of avoiding adverse weather and inadvertent entry into instrument meteorological conditions (IMC).
4. Explains courses of action to safely exit from an inadvertent IMC encounter.

D. TASK: CROSS-COUNTRY FLIGHT PLANNING (PPCL and PPCS)

REFERENCES: 14 CFR part 91; FAA-H-8083-25, FAA-H-8083-29; AC 61-84; Navigation Charts; A/FD; AIM.

Objective. To determine that the applicant:

1. Exhibits knowledge of the elements related to cross-country flight planning appropriate to the category/class aircraft.
2. Uses appropriate and current aeronautical charts.
3. Properly identifies airspace, obstructions, and terrain features.
4. Selects easily identifiable en route checkpoints, as appropriate.
5. Selects most favorable altitudes considering weather conditions and equipment capabilities.
6. Determines headings, flight time, and fuel requirements.
7. Selects appropriate navigation system/facilities and communication frequencies, if so equipped.
8. Applies pertinent information from NOTAMs, A/FD, and other flight publications.
9. Completes a navigation plan and simulates filing a VFR flight plan.

E. TASK: NATIONAL AIRSPACE SYSTEM (PPCL and PPCS)

REFERENCES: 14 CFR parts 71, 91; Navigation Charts; FAA-H-8083-29; AIM.

Objective. To determine that the applicant exhibits knowledge of the elements related to the National Airspace System by explaining:

1. Sport pilot privileges applicable to the following classes of airspace:

   a. Class B.
   b. Class C.
   c. Class D.
   d. Class E.
   e. Class G.

2. Special use and other airspace areas.
3. Temporary flight restrictions (TFRs).

F. TASK: OPERATION OF SYSTEMS (PPCL and PPCS)

REFERENCES: FAA-H-8083-25, FAA-H-8038-29; Aircraft Flight Manual/ POH.

Objective. To determine that the applicant exhibits knowledge of the elements related to the operation of systems on the light-sport aircraft provided for the flight test by explaining at least three (3) of the following systems, if applicable:

1. Canopy/riser and control system.
2. Flight instruments and engine instruments.
3. Landing gear.
4. Engine and propeller.
5. Fuel, oil, electrical and coolant system (if liquid cooled).
6. Avionics and auxiliary equipment, as installed.

G. TASK: AEROMEDICAL FACTORS (PPCL and PPCS)

REFERENCES: FAA-H-8083-25, FAA-H-8083-29; AIM.

Objective. To determine that the applicant exhibits knowledge of the elements related to aeromedical factors by explaining:

1. The effects of alcohol, drugs, and over-the-counter medications.
2. The symptoms, causes, effects, and corrective actions of at least three (3) of the following—

    a. hypoxia.
    b. hyperventilation.
    c. middle ear and sinus problems.
    d. spatial disorientation.
    e. motion sickness.
    f. stress and fatigue.
    g. dehydration.
    h. hypothermia

H. TASK: WATER AND POWERED PARACHUTE—SEA CHARACTERISTICS (PPCS)

REFERENCE: FAA-H-8083-23.

Objective. To determine that the applicant exhibits knowledge of the elements related to water and powered parachute—sea characteristics by explaining:

1. The characteristics of a water surface as affected by features, such as—

    a. size and location.
    b. protected and unprotected areas.
    c. surface wind.
    d. direction and strength of water current.
    e. floating and partially submerged debris.
    f. sandbars, islands, and shoals.
    g. vessel traffic and wakes.
    h. other features peculiar to the area.

2. Float and hull construction, and their effect on aircraft performance.
3. Causes of porpoising and skipping, and the pilot action required to prevent or correct these occurrences.

I. TASK: SEAPLANE BASES, MARITIME RULES, AND AIDS TO MARINE NAVIGATION (PPCS)

REFERENCES: FAA-H-8083-23; AIM.

Objective.   To determine that the applicant exhibits knowledge of the elements related to seaplane bases, maritime rules, and aids to marine navigation by explaining:

1. How to locate and identify seaplane bases on charts or in directories.
2. Operating restrictions at seaplane bases, if applicable.
3. Right-of-way, steering, and sailing rules pertinent to seaplane operation.
4. Marine navigation aids such as buoys, beacons, lights, and sound signals.

J. TASK: PERFORMANCE AND LIMITATIONS (PPCL and PPCS)

REFERENCES: FAA-H-8083-1, FAA-H-8032-29.

Objective.   To determine the applicant:

1. Exhibits knowledge of the elements related to performance and limitations by explaining the effects of temperature, altitude, humidity, and wind.
2. Determines if weight and center of gravity is within limits.
3. Describes the effects of atmospheric conditions on the PPC's performance and limitations.
4. Explains the effects and hazards of high winds, referencing the ground speed, high rates of turn, and power requirements on making downwind turns in close proximity to the ground.

K. TASK: PRINCIPLES OF FLIGHT (PPCL and PPCS)

REFERENCES: FAA-H-8083-1, FAA-H-8083-29.

Objective.   To determine the applicant exhibits knowledge of at least three (3) of the following aerodynamic principles:

1. Aerodynamics with respect to steering.
2. Propeller/Engine Torque Compensation.
3. Pendulum effect in PPCs.
4. Load factor effects in level flight and turns.
5. Wing flaring characteristics.
6. Explain the characteristics of improper chute rigging.

II. AREA OF OPERATION: PREFLIGHT PROCEDURES

NOTE: For single-seat applicants, the examiner shall select at least TASKs A, B, C, E, and for PPCS, TASK F.

A. TASK: PREFLIGHT INSPECTION (PPCL and PPCS)

REFERENCES: FAA-H-8038-29; Aircraft Flight Manual/POH.

Objective. To determine that the applicant:

1. Exhibits knowledge of the elements related to preflight inspection. This shall include which items must be inspected, the reasons for checking each item, and how to detect possible defects.
2. Inspects the powered parachute with reference to an appropriate checklist, or procedure.
3. Ensures that risers are properly attached and the chute is properly trimmed.
4. Verifies the powered parachute is in condition for safe flight.

B. TASK: CANOPY LAYOUT (PPCL and PPCS)

REFERENCES: FAA-H-8083-29; Aircraft Flight Manual/POH.

Objective. To determine that the applicant:

1. Exhibits knowledge of the elements of canopy layout.
2. Explains how to identify a line-over and demonstrates how to remove a line-over.
3. Verifies that canopy and riser system is laid out properly and in condition for inflation.
4. Demonstrates the ability to untwist twisted canopy suspension/ steering lines.
5. Verifies suspension and steering lines are not tangled or twisted.

C. TASK: ENGINE WARM UP/STARTING (PPCL and PPCS)

REFERENCES: FAA-H-8083-29; Aircraft Flight Manual/POH.

Objective. To determine that the applicant:

1. Exhibits knowledge of the elements related to recommended engine starting/warm up procedures.
2. Positions the powered parachute properly considering structures, surface conditions, other aircraft, and the safety of nearby persons and property.

D. TASK: COCKPIT MANAGEMENT (PPCL and PPCS)

REFERENCES: FAA-H-8083-25, FAA-H-8083-29; Aircraft Flight Manual/ POH.

Objective. To determine that the applicant:

1. Exhibits knowledge of the elements related to cockpit management procedures.
2. Ensures all loose items in the cockpit are secured.
3. Organizes material and equipment in an efficient manner so they are readily available.
4. Briefs occupant on the use of safety belts, shoulder harnesses, methods of egress, and other emergency procedures.

E. TASK: TAXIING (CANOPY INFLATED) (PPCL and PPCS)

REFERENCES: FAA-H-8083-29; Aircraft Flight Manual/POH.

Objective. To determine that the applicant:

1. Exhibits knowledge of the elements of taxiing with canopy inflated.
2. Positions PPC properly for existing wind conditions.
3. Monitors position and shape of canopy/riser system during taxi.
4. Centers the chute using power and steering as required.
5. Avoids other aircraft and ground hazards.
6. Controls direction and speed for 100 feet of forward movement.
7. Completes proper engine shutdown and canopy deflation procedure.

F. TASK: TAXIING AND SAILING (PPCS)

REFERENCES: FAA-H-8083-3; USCG Navigation Rules; International-Inland; Aircraft Flight Manual/POH.

Objective. To determine that the applicant:

1. Exhibits knowledge of the elements related to water taxi and sailing procedures.
2. Makes smooth and appropriate throttle applications as the canopy transitions from ground pickup through maximum drag to water taxi position.
3. Plans and follows the most favorable course while taxiing or sailing considering wind, water current, water conditions, and maritime regulations.
4. Uses the appropriate idle, plow, or step taxi technique.
5. Uses flight controls, water rudder, and power correctly so as to follow the desired course while sailing.
6. Prevents and corrects for porpoising and skipping.
7. Avoids other aircraft, vessels, and hazards.
8. Complies with PPC base signs, signals, and clearances.

G. TASK: BEFORE TAKEOFF CHECK (PPCL and PPCS)

REFERENCES: FAA-H-8083-3, FAA-H-8083-29; Aircraft Flight Manual/POH.

Objective. To determine that the applicant:

1. Exhibits knowledge of the elements related to the before takeoff check. This shall include the reasons for checking each item and how to detect malfunctions.
2. Reviews takeoff performance, takeoff distances, departure, and emergency procedures.
3. Positions the powered parachute properly considering wind, other aircraft, and surface conditions.
4. Ensures that engine temperature is suitable for run-up and takeoff.
5. Ensures the powered parachute is in safe operating condition.
6. Avoids runway incursions and/or ensures no conflict with traffic.

III. AREA OF OPERATION: AIRPORT AND SEAPLANE BASE OPERATIONS

A. TASK: RADIO COMMUNICATIONS (PPCL and PPCS)

NOTE: If the aircraft is not radio equipped, this TASK shall be tested orally for procedures ONLY.

REFERENCES: 14 CFR part 91; FAA-H-8083-25, FAA-H-8083-29; AIM.

Objective. To determine that the applicant:

1. Exhibits knowledge of the elements related to radio communications at airports without operating control towers.
2. Selects appropriate frequencies.
3. Transmits using recommended phraseology.
4. Receives, acknowledges and complies with radio communications and complies with instructions.

B. TASK: TRAFFIC PATTERNS (PPCL and PPCS)

REFERENCES: FAA-H-8083-3, FAA-H-8083-25, FAA-H-8083-29; AC 90-66; AIM.

Objective. To determine that the applicant:

1. Exhibits knowledge of the elements related to traffic patterns and shall include procedures at airports with and without operating control towers, prevention of runway incursions, collision avoidance, wake turbulence avoidance, and wind shear.
2. Complies with proper local traffic pattern procedures.
3. Maintains proper spacing from other aircraft.
4. Corrects for wind drift to maintain the proper ground track.
5. Maintains orientation with the runway/landing area in use.
6. Maintains traffic pattern altitude, ±100 feet.

C. TASK: AIRPORT RUNWAY MARKINGS AND LIGHTING (PPCL and PPCS)

REFERENCES: FAA-H-8083-23, FAA-H-8083-25, FAA-H-8083-29; AIM.

Objective. To determine that the applicant:

1. Exhibits knowledge of the elements related to airport/seaplane base, markings and lighting with emphasis on runway incursion avoidance.
2. Properly identifies and interprets airport/seaplane base markings and lighting.

IV. AREA OF OPERATION: TAKEOFFS, LANDINGS, AND GO-AROUNDS

NOTE: For single-seat applicants, the examiner shall select all TASKs.

A. TASK: NORMAL TAKEOFF AND CLIMB (PPCL and PPCS)

REFERENCES: FAA-H-8083-3,   FAA-H-8083-23,   FAA-H-8083-29; Aircraft Flight Manual/POH.

Objective.   To determine that the applicant:

1. Exhibits knowledge of the elements related to normal takeoff and climb operations and rejected takeoff procedures.
2. Clears the area.
3. Divides attention inside and outside the cockpit.
4. Makes smooth and appropriate throttle applications as the canopy transitions from ground pickup through maximum drag to taxi position.
5. Checks canopy, ensuring that all end cells are fully inflated and canopy is centered, lines are free and unobstructed and in condition for takeoff.
6. Retracts the water rudders as appropriate, advances the throttle smoothly to takeoff power. (PPCS)
7. Establishes and maintains the most efficient planing/climb attitude and corrects for porpoising and skipping. (PPCS)
8. Maintains takeoff power to a safe maneuvering altitude.
9. Maintains directional control and proper wind-drift correction throughout the takeoff and climb.
10. Complies with noise abatement procedures.

B. TASK: NORMAL APPROACH AND LANDING (PPCL and PPCS)

NOTE: The applicant's knowledge of minimizing crosswind elements shall be evaluated through oral testing.

REFERENCES: FAA-H-8083-3, FAA-H-8083-23, FAA-H-8083-29; Aircraft Flight Manual/POH.

Objective. To determine that the applicant:

1. Exhibits knowledge of the elements related to a normal approach and landing.
2. Adequately surveys the intended landing area. (PPCS)
3. Considers the wind conditions, landing surface, obstructions, and selects a suitable touchdown point.
4. Establishes the recommended approach and landing configuration and adjusts power as required.
5. Maintains a stabilized approach.
6. Makes smooth, timely, and correct control application during the flare and touchdown.
7. Contacts the water at the proper pitch attitude. (PPCS)
8. Touches down smoothly. (PPCS)
9. Maintains directional control throughout the approach and landing sequence and touchdown.
10. Completes proper engine shutdown and canopy deflation procedure.

C. TASK: GLASSY WATER TAKEOFF AND CLIMB (PPCS)

NOTE: If glassy water condition does not exist, the applicant shall be evaluated by simulating the TASK.

REFERENCES: FAA-H-8083-3, FAA-H-8083-23; Aircraft Flight Manual/ POH.

Objective.   To determine that the applicant:

1. Exhibits knowledge of the elements related to glassy water takeoff and climb.
2. Clears the area; selects an appropriate takeoff path considering surface hazards and/or vessels and surface conditions.
3. Retracts the water rudders as appropriate; advances the throttle smoothly to takeoff power.
4. Establishes and maintains an appropriate planing attitude, directional control, and corrects for porpoising, skipping, and increases in water drag.
5. Utilizes appropriate techniques to lift PPCS from the water considering surface conditions.
6. Establishes proper attitude.
7. Maintains takeoff power to a safe maneuvering altitude.
8. Maintains directional control and proper wind-drift correction throughout takeoff and climb.

D. TASK: GLASSY WATER APPROACH AND LANDING (PPCS)

NOTE: If glassy water condition does not exist, the applicant shall be evaluated by simulating the TASK.

REFERENCES: FAA-H-8083-3, FAA-H-8083-25; Aircraft Flight Manual/ POH.

Objective.   To determine that the applicant:

1. Exhibits knowledge of the elements related to glassy water approach and landing.
2. Adequately surveys the intended landing area.
3. Considers the wind conditions, water depth, hazards, surrounding terrain, and other watercraft.
4. Selects the most suitable approach path and touchdown area.
5. Establishes the recommended approach and landing configuration, and adjusts power as required.
6. Makes smooth, timely, and correct power and control adjustments to maintain proper pitch attitude and rate of descent to touchdown.
7. Contacts the water in the proper pitch attitude. Maintains directional control throughout the approach and landing sequence.

E. TASK: ROUGH WATER TAKEOFF AND CLIMB (PPCS)

NOTE: If rough water condition does not exist, the applicant shall be evaluated by simulating the TASK.

REFERENCES: FAA-H-8083-3, FAA-H-8083-23; Aircraft Flight Manual/ POH.

Objective.   To determine that the applicant:

1. Exhibits knowledge of the elements related to rough water takeoff and climb.
2. Clears the area; selects an appropriate takeoff path considering wind, swells surface hazards, and/or vessels.
3. Retracts the water rudders as appropriate; advances the throttle smoothly to takeoff power.
4. Establishes and maintains an appropriate planing attitude, directional control, and corrects for porpoising, skipping, or excessive bouncing.
5. Maintains takeoff power to a safe maneuvering altitude.
6. Maintains directional control and proper wind-drift correction throughout takeoff and climb.

F. TASK: ROUGH WATER APPROACH AND LANDING (PPCS)

NOTE: If rough water condition does not exist, the applicant shall be evaluated by simulating the TASK.

REFERENCES: FAA-H-8083-3, FAA-H-8083-23; Aircraft Flight Manual/ POH.

Objective. To determine that the applicant:

1. Exhibits knowledge of the elements related to rough water approach and landing.
2. Adequately surveys the intended landing area.
3. Considers the wind conditions, water, depth, hazards, surrounding terrain, and other watercraft.
4. Selects the most suitable approach path and touchdown area.
5. Establishes the recommended approach and landing configuration, and adjusts power as required.
6. Makes smooth, timely, and correct power and control inputs during the roundout and touch down.
7. Contacts the water in the proper pitch attitude, considering the type of rough water.
8. Maintains directional control throughout the approach and landing sequence.

G. TASK: GO-AROUND/REJECTED LANDING (PPCL and PPCS)

REFERENCES: FAA-H-8083-3, FAA-H-8083-29; Aircraft Flight Manual/ POH.

Objective. To determine that the applicant:

1. Exhibits knowledge of the elements related to a go-around/ rejected landing.
2. Makes a timely decision to discontinue the approach to landing.
3. Applies takeoff power immediately.
4. Retracts the water rudders as appropriate, after a positive rate of climb is established. (PPCS)
5. Maneuvers to the side of the runway/landing area to clear and avoid conflicting traffic, if appropriate.
6. Maintains appropriate power to a safe maneuvering altitude.
7. Maintains directional control and proper wind-drift correction throughout the climb.

V. AREA OF OPERATION: PERFORMANCE MANEUVER

A. TASK: CONSTANT ALTITUDE TURNS (PPCL and PPCS)

REFERENCES: FAA-H-8083-3, FAA-H-8083-29.

Objective.   To determine that the applicant:

1. Exhibits knowledge of the elements related to constant altitude turns.
2. Plans the maneuver no lower than 200 feet AGL.
3. Rolls into a constant bank 360° turn.
4. Performs the task in the opposite direction, as specified by the examiner.
5. Divides attention between powered parachute control and orientation.
6. Maintains altitude, ±100 feet, and rolls out on the entry heading ±10°.

VI. AREA OF OPERATION: GROUND REFERENCE MANEUVERS

NOTE: The examiner shall select at least one ground reference maneuver.

NOTE: For single-seat applicants, the examiner shall select at least one ground reference maneuver.

A. TASK: RECTANGULAR COURSE (PPCL and PPCS)

REFERENCES: FAA-H-8083-3, FAA-H-8083-29.

Objective.   To determine that the applicant:

1. Exhibits knowledge of the elements related to a rectangular course.
2. Selects a suitable reference area, considering all obstacles.
3. Plans the maneuver so as to not descend below 200 feet above ground level at an appropriate distance from the selected reference area, 45° to the downwind leg.
4. Applies adequate wind-drift correction during straight-and-turning flight to maintain a constant ground track around the rectangular reference area.
5. Divides attention between powered parachute control and the ground track while maintaining coordinated flight.
6. Maintains altitude, ±100 feet.

B. TASK: S-TURNS (PPCL and PPCS)

REFERENCES: FAA-H-8083-3, FAA-H-8083-29.

Objective.   To determine that the applicant:

1. Exhibits knowledge of the elements related to S-turns.
2. Selects a suitable ground reference line, considering all obstacles.
3. Plans the maneuver so as to not descend below 200 feet above the ground.
4. Applies adequate wind-drift correction to track a constant radius turn on each side of the selected reference line.
5. Reverses the direction of turn directly over the selected reference line.
6. Divides attention between powered parachute control and the ground track while maintaining coordinated flight.
7. Maintains altitude, ±100 feet.

C. TASK: TURNS AROUND A POINT (PPCL and PPCS)

REFERENCES: FAA-H-8083-3, FAA-H-8083-29.

Objective. To determine that the applicant:

1. Exhibits knowledge of the elements related to turns around a point.
2. Selects a suitable ground reference point, considering all obstacles.
3. Plans the maneuver so as to not descend below 200 feet above the ground, at an appropriate distance from the reference point.
4. Applies adequate wind-drift correction to track a constant radius turn around the selected reference point.
5. Divides attention between powered parachute control and the ground track while maintaining coordinated flight.
6. Maintains altitude, ±100 feet.

VII. AREA OF OPERATION: NAVIGATION

A. TASK: PILOTAGE AND DEAD RECKONING

REFERENCE: FAA-H-8083-25, FAA-H-8083-29.

Objective. To determine that the applicant:

1. Exhibits knowledge of the elements related to pilotage and dead reckoning, as appropriate.
2. Follows the preplanned course by reference to landmarks.
3. Identifies landmarks by relating surface features to chart symbols.
4. Verifies the aircraft's position within 3 nautical miles of the flight-planned route.
5. Determines there is sufficient fuel to complete the planned flight, if not, has an alternate plan.
6. Maintains the appropriate altitude, ±200 feet and heading, ±15°.

B. TASK: DIVERSION

REFERENCES: FAA-H-8083-25, FAA-H-8083-29; AIM.

Objective. To determine that the applicant:

1. Exhibits knowledge of the elements related to diversion.
2. Selects an appropriate alternate airport or landing area and route.
3. Determines there is sufficient fuel to fly to the alternate airport or landing area.
4. Turns to and establishes a course to the selected alternate destination.
5. Maintains the appropriate altitude, ±200 feet, and heading, ±15°.

C. TASK: LOST PROCEDURES

REFERENCES: FAA-H-8083-25, FAA-H-8083-29; AIM.

Objective. To determine that the applicant:

1. Exhibits knowledge of the elements related to lost procedures.
2. Selects an appropriate course of action.
3. Maintains an appropriate heading and climbs if necessary.
4. Identifies prominent landmarks.
5. Uses navigation systems/facilities and or contacts an ATC facility for assistance, as appropriate.

VIII. AREA OF OPERATION: EMERGENCY OPERATIONS

NOTE: For single-seat applicants, the examiner shall select TASK A.

A. TASK: EMERGENCY APPROACH AND LANDING (SIMULATED) (PPCL and PPCS)

REFERENCES: FAA-H-8083-3, FAA-H-8083-23, FAA-H-8083-29; Aircraft Flight Manual/POH.

Objective. To determine that the applicant:

1. Exhibits knowledge of the elements related to emergency approach and landing procedures.
2. Analyzes the situation and selects an appropriate course of action.
3. Plans and follows a flight pattern to the selected landing area considering altitude, wind, terrain, and obstructions.
4. Prepares for landing or go-around, as specified by the examiner.

B. TASK: SYSTEMS AND EQUIPMENT MALFUNCTIONS (PPCL and PPCS)

REFERENCES: FAA-H-8083-3, FAA-H-8083-23, FAA-H-8083-29; Aircraft Flight Manual/POH.

Objective. To determine that the applicant:

1. Exhibits knowledge of the elements related to causes, indications, and pilot actions for various systems and equipment malfunctions.
2. Analyzes the situation and takes action, appropriate to the aircraft used for the practical test, in at least three (3) of the following areas, if applicable—

   a. engine/oil and fuel.
   b. electrical.
   c. carburetor or induction icing.
   d. smoke and/or fire.
   e. flight control/trim.
   f. propeller.
   g. any other emergency unique to the powered parachute flown.

C. TASK: EMERGENCY EQUIPMENT AND SURVIVAL GEAR (PPCL and PPCS)

REFERENCES: AC 91-13, AC 91-58, AC 91-69; FAA-H-8083-3, FAA-H-8083-23, FAA-H-8083-29; Aircraft Flight Manual; POH; AIM.

Objective. To determine that the applicant exhibits knowledge of the elements related to emergency equipment appropriate to the following environmental conditions:

1. Mountainous terrain.
2. Large bodies of water.
3. Desert conditions.
4. Extreme temperature changes.

IX. AREA OF OPERATION: POSTFLIGHT PROCEDURES

NOTE: For single-seat applicants, the examiner shall select TASK A and all other TASKs as applicable.

A. TASK: AFTER LANDING, PARKING, AND SECURING (PPCL and PPCS)

REFERENCES: FAA-H-8083-3, FAA-H-8083-23, FAA-H-8083-29; Aircraft Flight Manual/POH.

Objective. To determine that the applicant:

1. Exhibits knowledge of the elements related to after landing, parking, and securing procedures.
2. Observes runway hold lines and other surface control markings and lighting.
3. Parks in an appropriate area, considering the safety of nearby persons and property.
4. Follows the appropriate procedure for engine shutdown.
5. Protects canopy/riser system from the hot engine while stowing/ securing.

B. TASK: ANCHORING (PPCS)

REFERENCES: FAA-H-8083-3, FAA-H-8083-23; Aircraft Flight Manual/ POH.

Objective. To determine that the applicant:

1. Exhibits knowledge of the elements related to anchoring.
2. Selects a suitable area for anchoring, considering PPCS's movement, water depth, tide, wind, and weather changes.
3. Uses an adequate number of anchors and lines of sufficient strength and length to ensure the PPCS's security.

C. TASK: DOCKING AND MOORING (PPCS)

REFERENCES: FAA-H-8083-3, FAA-H-8083-23; Aircraft Flight Manual/ POH.

Objective. To determine that the applicant:

1. Exhibits knowledge of the elements related to docking and mooring.
2. Approaches the dock or mooring buoy in the proper direction considering speed hazards, wind, and water current.
3. Ensures PPCS security.

D. TASK: RAMPING/BEACHING (PPCS)

REFERENCES: FAA-H-8083-3, FAA-H-8083-23; Aircraft Flight Manual/ POH.

Objective. To determine that the applicant:

1. Exhibits knowledge of the elements related to ramping/beaching.
2. Approaches the ramp/beach considering persons and property, in the proper attitude and direction, at a safe speed, considering water depth, tide, current, and wind.
3. Ramps/beaches and secures the PPCS in a manner that will protect it from the harmful effect of wind, waves, and changes in water level.

SECTION 3

SPORT PILOT

FLIGHT INSTRUCTOR

SECTION 3—CONTENTS

FLIGHT INSTRUCTOR

CHECKLISTS

FLIGHT INSTRUCTOR CERTIFICATE WITH SPORT PILOT PRIVILEGES

AREAS OF OPERATION

APPLICANT'S PRACTICAL TEST CHECKLIST

APPOINTMENT WITH EXAMINER:

EXAMINER'S NAME _____

LOCATION _____

DATE/TIME _____

ACCEPTABLE AIRCRAFT

- ☐ Aircraft Documents: Airworthiness Certificate
- ☐ Registration Certificate
- ☐ Aircraft Maintenance Records: Airworthiness Inspections/Safety Directives
- ☐ Pilot's Operating Handbook or FAA-Approved Flight Manual or Manufacturer's Operating Instructions

PERSONAL EQUIPMENT

- ☐ Current Aeronautical Charts
- ☐ Computer and Plotter
- ☐ Flight Plan Form
- ☐ Flight Logs
- ☐ Current AIM
- ☐ Current Airport Facility Directory

PERSONAL RECORDS

- ☐ Identification—Photo/Signature ID
- ☐ Pilot Certificate
- ☐ Medical Certificate or Driver's License
- ☐ Completed FAA Form 8710-11, Application for an Airman Certificate and/or Rating—Sport Pilot
- ☐ Airman Knowledge Test Report
- ☐ Logbook with Instructor's Endorsement
- ☐ FAA Form 8060-5, Notice of Disapproval (if applicable)
- ☐ Examiner's Fee (if applicable)

EXAMINER'S PRACTICAL TEST CHECKLIST FOR FLIGHT INSTRUCTOR—WEIGHT SHIFT CONTROL

APPLICANT'S NAME _____

LOCATION _____

DATE/TIME _____

I. FUNDAMENTAL OF INSTRUCTING

Note: The examiner must select TASK F and one other TASK.

- ☐ A. The Learning Process
- ☐ B. Human Behavior and Effective Communication
- ☐ C. The Teaching Process
- ☐ D. Teaching Methods
- ☐ E. Critique and Evaluation
- ☐ **F. Flight Instructor Characteristics and Responsibilities**
- ☐ G. Planning Instructional Activity

II. TECHNICAL SUBJECT AREAS

Note: The examiner must select TASK D and one other TASK.

- ☐ A. Aeromedical Factors
- ☐ B. Visual Scanning and Collision Avoidance
- ☐ C. Federal Aviation Regulations and Publications
- ☐ **D. Logbook Entries and Certificate Endorsements**

III. PREFLIGHT LESSON ON A MANEUVER TO BE PERFORMED IN FLIGHT

Note: The examiner must select one maneuver TASK.

- ☐ **Maneuver Lesson**

Instructor applicants must be tested in the following areas of operation appropriate to the aircraft category/class instructor privileges they seek (Refer to the appropriate category/class section of the PTS). Notes listed under each area of operation identify the TASKs that must be tested. In some cases the specific TASK is identified, in other cases a minimum number of TASKs are identified.

AREAS OF OPERATION

I. PREFLIGHT PREPARATION

Note: The examiner must select TASKs J and K and two other TASKs.

- ☐ A. Certificates and Documents (WSCL and WSCS)
- ☐ B. Airworthiness Requirements (WSCL and WSCS)
- ☐ C. Weather Information (WSCL and WSCS)
- ☐ D. Cross-Country Flight Planning (WSCL and WSCS)
- ☐ E. National Airspace System (WSCL and WSCS)
- ☐ F. Operation of Systems (WSCL and WSCS)
- ☐ G. Aeromedical Factors (WSCL and WSCS)
- ☐ H. Water and Seaplane Characteristics (WSCS)
- ☐ I. Seaplane Bases, Maritime Rules, and Aids To Marine Navigation (WSCS)
- ☐ **J. Performance and Limitations (WSCL and WSCS)**
- ☐ **K. Principles of Flight (WSCL and WSCS)**

II. PREFLIGHT PROCEDURES

Note: The examiner must select two TASKs.

- ☐ A. Assembly (WSCL and WSCS)
- ☐ B. Wing Tuning (WSCL and WSCS)
- ☐ C. Preflight Inspection (WSCL and WSCS)
- ☐ D. Cockpit Management (WSCL and WSCS)
- ☐ E. Engine Starting (WSCL and WSCS)
- ☐ F. Taxiing (WSCL)
- ☐ G. Taxiing and Sailing (WSCS)
- ☐ H. Before Takeoff Check (WSCL and WSCS)

III. AIRPORT AND SEAPLANE BASE OPERATIONS

Note: The examiner must select one TASK.

- ☐ A. Radio Communications (WSCL and WSCS)
- ☐ B. Traffic Patterns (WSCL and WSCS)
- ☐ C. Airport Runway Markings and Lighting (WSCL and WSCS)

IV. TAKEOFFS, LANDINGS, AND GO-AROUNDS

Note: The examiner must select TASK H and one takeoff/landing TASK.

- ☐ A. Normal and Crosswind Takeoff and Climb (WSCL and WSCS)
- ☐ B. Power-on and Crosswind Approach and Landing (WSCL and WSCS)
- ☐ C. Glassy Water Takeoff and Climb (WSCS)
- ☐ D. Glassy Water Approach and Landing (WSCS)
- ☐ E. Rough Water Takeoff and Climb (WSCS)
- ☐ F. Rough Water Approach and Landing (WSCS)
- ☐ G. Steep Approach to a Landing (WSCL and WSCS)
- ☐ **H. Go-Around/Rejected Landing (WSCL and WSCS)**

V. PERFORMANCE MANEUVER

Note: The examiner must select TASK A.

- ☐ **A. Steep Turns (WSCL and WSCS)**

VI. GROUND REFERENCE MANEUVERS

Note: The examiner must select one TASK.

- ☐ A. Rectangular Course (WSCL and WSCS)
- ☐ B. S-Turns (WSCL and WSCS)
- ☐ C. Turns Around a Point (WSCL and WSCS)

VII. NAVIGATION

Note: The examiner must select one TASK.

- ☐ A. Pilotage and Dead Reckoning (WSCL and WSCS)
- ☐ B. Diversion (WSCL and WSCS)
- ☐ C. Lost Procedures (WSCL and WSCS)

VIII. SLOW FLIGHT AND STALL

Note: The examiner must select TASK C and one other TASK.

- ☐ A. Maneuvering During Slow Flight (WSCL and WSCS)
- ☐ B. Power-off Stall (WSCL and WSCS)
- ☐ **C. Whip Stall and Tumble Awareness (WSCL and WSCS)**

IX. EMERGENCY OPERATIONS

Note: The examiner must select TASK A, and one other other task for WSCs.

☐ **A. Emergency Approach and Landing (Simulated) (WSCL and WSCS)**
☐ B. Systems and Equipment Malfunctions (WSCL and WSCS)
☐ C. Emergency Equipment and Survival Gear (WSCL and WSCS)

X. POSTFLIGHT PROCEDURES

Note: The examiner must select TASK A, and one other TASK for WSCS.

☐ **A. After Landing, Parking, and Securing (WSCL and WSCS)**
☐ B. Anchoring (WSCS)
☐ C. Docking and Mooring (WSCS)
☐ D. Ramping/Beaching (WSCS)

INSTRUCTOR'S PROFICIENCY CHECK CHECKLIST FOR FLIGHT INSTRUCTOR—WEIGHT SHIFT CONTROL

APPLICANT'S NAME _____

LOCATION _____

DATE/TIME _____

I.   FUNDAMENTALS OF INSTRUCTING

Note: The instructor may select any of the below listed FOI TASKs for a proficiency check. However, the TASKs are not required on a proficiency check.

- ☐   A.   The Learning Process
- ☐   B.   Human Behavior and Effective Communication
- ☐   C.   The Teaching Process
- ☐   D.   Teaching Methods
- ☐   E.   Critique and Evaluation
- ☐   F.   Flight Instructor Characteristics and Responsibilities
- ☐   G.   Planning Instructional Activity

II.   TECHNICAL SUBJECT AREAS

Note: The instructor must select TASK D and one other TASK.

- ☐   A.   Aeromedical Factors
- ☐   B.   Visual Scanning and Collision Avoidance
- ☐   C.   Federal Aviation Regulations and Publications
- ☐   **D.   Logbook Entries and Certificate Endorsements**

III.   PREFLIGHT LESSON ON A MANEUVER TO BE PERFORMED IN FLIGHT

Note: The instructor must select one maneuver TASK.

- ☐   **Maneuver Lesson**

Instructor applicants must be tested in the following areas of operation appropriate to the aircraft category/class instructor privileges they seek (Refer to the appropriate category/class section of the PTS). Notes listed under each area of operation identify the TASKs that must be tested. In some cases the specific TASK is identified, in other cases a minimum number of TASKs are identified.

SEE SECTION 1 OF THE PTS

AREAS OF OPERATION

I. PREFLIGHT PREPARATION

Note: The instructor must select TASKs F and K.

- ☐ A. Certificates and Documents (WSCL and WSCS)
- ☐ B. Airworthiness Requirements (WSCL and WSCS)
- ☐ C. Weather Information (WSCL and WSCS)
- ☐ D. Cross-Country Flight Planning (WSCL and WSCS)
- ☐ E. National Airspace System (WSCL and WSCS)
- ☐ **F. Operation of Systems (WSCL and WSCS)**
- ☐ G. Aeromedical Factors (WSCL and WSCS)
- ☐ H. Water and Seaplane Characteristics (WSCS)
- ☐ I. Seaplane Bases, Maritime Rules, and Aids To Marine Navigation (WSCS)
- ☐ J. Performance and Limitations (WSCL and WSCS)
- ☐ **K. Principles of Flight (WSCL and WSCS)**

II. PREFLIGHT PROCEDURES

Note: The instructor must select two TASKs.

- ☐ A. Assembly (WSCL and WSCS)
- ☐ B. Wing Tuning (WSCL and WSCS)
- ☐ C. Preflight Inspection (WSCL and WSCS)
- ☐ D. Cockpit Management (WSCL and WSCS)
- ☐ E. Engine Starting (WSCL and WSCS)
- ☐ F. Taxiing (WSCL)
- ☐ G. Taxiing and Sailing (WSCS)
- ☐ H. Before Takeoff Check (WSCL and WSCS)

III. AIRPORT AND SEAPLANE BASE OPERATIONS

Note: The instructor must select TASK C.

- ☐ A. Radio Communications (WSCL and WSCS)
- ☐ B. Traffic Patterns (WSCL and WSCS)
- ☐ **C. Airport Runway Markings and Lighting (WSCL and WSCS)**

IV. TAKEOFFS, LANDINGS, AND GO-AROUNDS

Note: The instructor must select TASK H and one takeoff/ landing TASK.

☐   A.   Normal and Crosswind Takeoff and Climb (WSCL and WSCS)
☐   B.   Power-on and Crosswind Approach and Landing (WSCL and WSCS)
☐   C.   Glassy Water Takeoff and Climb (WSCS)
☐   D.   Glassy Water Approach and Landing (WSCS)
☐   E.   Rough Water Takeoff and Climb (WSCS)
☐   F.   Rough Water Approach and Landing (WSCS)
☐   G.   Steep Approach to a Landing (WSCL and WSCS)
☐   **H.**   **Go-around/Rejected Landing (WSCL and WSCS)**

V. PERFORMANCE MANEUVER

Note: The instructor must select TASK A.

☐   **A.**   **Steep Turns (WSCL and WSCS)**

VI. GROUND REFERENCE MANEUVERS

Note: The instructor must select one TASK.

☐   A.   Rectangular Course (WSCL and WSCS)
☐   B.   S-Turns (WSCL and WSCS)
☐   C.   Turns Around a Point (WSCL and WSCS)

VII. NAVIGATION

Note: The instructor must select one TASK.

☐   A.   Pilotage and Dead Reckoning (WSCL and WSCS)
☐   B.   Diversion (WSCL and WSCS)
☐   C.   Lost Procedures (WSCL and WSCS)

VIII. SLOW FLIGHT AND STALL

Note: The instructor must select TASK C and one other TASK.

☐   A.   Maneuvering During Slow Flight (WSCL and WSCS)
☐   B.   Power-off Stall (WSCL and WSCS)
☐   **C.**   **Whip Stall and Tumble Awareness (WSCL and WSCS)**

IX.   EMERGENCY OPERATIONS

Note: The instructor must select TASK A.

☐   **A.   Emergency Approach and Landing (Simulated) (WSCL and WSCS)**
☐   B.   Systems and Equipment Malfunctions (WSCL and WSCS)
☐   C.   Emergency Equipment and Survival Gear (WSCL and WSCS)

X.   POSTFLIGHT PROCEDURES

Note: The instructor must select TASK A and one other TASK for WSCS.

☐   **A.   After Landing, Parking, and Securing (WSCL and WSCS)**
☐   B.   Anchoring (WSCS)
☐   C.   Docking and Mooring (WSCS)
☐   D.   Ramping/Beaching (WSCS)

EXAMINER'S PRACTICAL TEST CHECKLIST FOR FLIGHT INSTRUCTOR—POWERED PARACHUTE

APPLICANT'S NAME_____

LOCATION_____

DATE/TIME_____

I.   FUNDAMENTALS OF INSTRUCTING

Note: The examiner must select TASK F and one other TASK.

- ☐   A.   The Learning Process
- ☐   B.   Human Behavior and Effective Communication
- ☐   C.   The Teaching Process
- ☐   D.   Teaching Methods
- ☐   E.   Critique and Evaluation
- ☐   **F.   Flight Instructor Characteristics and Responsibilities**
- ☐   G.   Planning Instructional Activity

II.   TECHNICAL SUBJECT AREAS

Note: The examiner must select TASK D and one other TASK.

- ☐   A.   Aeromedical Factors
- ☐   B.   Visual Scanning and Collision Avoidance
- ☐   C.   Federal Aviation Regulations and Publications
- ☐   **D.   Logbook Entries and Certificate Endorsements**

III.   PREFLIGHT LESSON ON A MANEUVER TO BE PERFORMED IN FLIGHT

Note: The examiner must select one maneuver TASK.

- ☐   **Maneuver Lesson**

Instructor applicants must be tested in the following areas of operation appropriate to the aircraft category/class instructor privileges they seek (Refer to the appropriate category/class section of the PTS). Notes listed under each area of operation identify the TASKs that must be tested. In some cases the specific TASK is identified, in other cases a minimum number of TASKs are identified.

SEE SECTION 2 OF THE PTS

AREAS OF OPERATION

I.   PREFLIGHT PREPARATION

Note: The examiner must select TASKs J and K and two other TASKs.

- ☐   A.   Certificates and Documents (PPCL and PPCS)
- ☐   B.   Airworthiness Requirements (PPCL and PPCS)
- ☐   C.   Weather Information (PPCL and PPCS)
- ☐   D.   Cross-Country Flight Planning (PPCL and PPCS)
- ☐   E.   National Airspace System (PPCL and PPCS)
- ☐   F.   Operation of Systems (PPCL and PPCS)
- ☐   G.   Aeromedical Factors (PPCL and PPCS)
- ☐   H.   Water and Seaplane Characteristics (PPCS)
- ☐   I.   Seaplane Bases, Maritime Rules, and Aids to Marine Navigation (PPCS)
- ☐   **J.   Performance and Limitations (PPCL and PPCS)**
- ☐   **K.   Principles of Flight (PPCL and PPCS)**

II.   PREFLIGHT PROCEDURES

Note: The examiner must select TASKs B and E.

- ☐   A.   Preflight Inspection (PPCL and PPCS)
- ☐   **B.   Canopy Layout (PPCL and PPCS)**
- ☐   C.   Engine Warm Up/Starting (PPCL and PPCS)
- ☐   D.   Cockpit Management (PPCL and PPCS)
- ☐   **E.   Taxiing (Canopy Inflated) (PPCL and PPCS)**
- ☐   F.   Taxiing and Sailing (PPCS)
- ☐   G.   Before Takeoff Check (PPCL and PPCS)

III.   AIRPORT AND SEAPLANE BASE OPERATIONS

Note: The examiner must select one TASK.

- ☐   A.   Radio Communications (PPCL and PPCS)
- ☐   B.   Traffic Patterns (PPCL and PPCS)
- ☐   C.   Airport Runway Markings and Lighting (PPCL and PPCS)

IV. TAKEOFFS, LANDINGS, AND GO-AROUNDS

Note: The examiner must select TASK G and one takeoff/landing TASK.

- ☐ A. Normal Takeoff and Climb (PPCL and PPCS)
- ☐ B. Normal Approach and Landing (PPCL and PPCS)
- ☐ C. Glassy Water Takeoff and Climb (PPCS)
- ☐ D. Glassy Water Approach and Landing (PPCS)
- ☐ E. Rough Water Takeoff and Climb (PPCS)
- ☐ F. Rough Water Approach and Landing (PPCS)
- ☐ **G. Go-around/Rejected Landing (PPCL and PPCS)**

V. PERFORMANCE MANEUVER

Note: The examiner must select TASK A.

- ☐ **A. Constant Altitude Turns (PPCL and PPCS)**

VI. GROUND REFERENCE MANEUVERS

Note: The examiner must select one TASK.

- ☐ A. Rectangular Course (PPCL and PPCS)
- ☐ B. S-Turns (PPCL and PPCS)
- ☐ C. Turns Around a Point (PPCL and PPCS)

VII. NAVIGATION

Note: The examiner must select one TASK.

- ☐ A. Pilotage and Dead Reckoning (PPCL and PPCS)
- ☐ B. Diversion (PPCL and PPCS)
- ☐ C. Lost Procedures (PPCL and PPCS)

VIII. EMERGENCY OPERATIONS

Note: The examiner must select TASK A and one other TASK.

- ☐ **A. Emergency Approach and Landing (Simulated) (PPCL and PPCS)**
- ☐ B. Systems and Equipment Malfunctions (PPCL and PPCS)
- ☐ C. Emergency Equipment and Survival Gear (PPCL and PPCS)

IX. POSTFLIGHT PROCEDURES

Note: The examiner must select TASK A and one other TASK for PPCS.

☐ **A. After Landing, Parking, and Securing (PPCL and PPCS)**
☐ B. Anchoring (PPCS)
☐ C. Docking and Mooring (PPCS)
☐ D. Ramping/Beaching (PPCS)

INSTRUCTOR'S PROFICIENCY CHECK CHECKLIST FOR FLIGHT INSTRUCTOR—POWERED PARACHUTE

APPLICANT'S NAME _____

LOCATION _____

DATE/TIME _____

I.   FUNDAMENTALS OF INSTRUCTING

Note: The instructor may select any of the below listed FOI TASKs for a proficiency check. However, these TASKs are not required on a proficiency check.

- ☐   A.   The Learning Process
- ☐   B.   Human Behavior and Effective Communication
- ☐   C.   The Teaching Process
- ☐   D.   Teaching Methods
- ☐   E.   Critique and Evaluation
- ☐   F.   Flight Instructor Characteristics and Responsibilities
- ☐   G.   Planning Instructional Activity

II.   TECHNICAL SUBJECT AREAS

Note: The examiner must select TASK D and one other TASK.

- ☐   A.   Aeromedical Factors
- ☐   B.   Visual Scanning and Collision Avoidance
- ☐   C.   Federal Aviation Regulations and Publications
- ☐   **D.   Logbook Entries and Certificate Endorsements**

III.   PREFLIGHT LESSON ON A MANEUVER TO BE PERFORMED IN FLIGHT

Note: The examiner must select one maneuver TASK.

- ☐   **Maneuver Lesson**

Instructor applicants must be tested in the following areas of operation appropriate to the aircraft category/class instructor privileges they seek (Refer to the appropriate category/class section of the PTS). Notes listed under each area of operation identify the TASKs that must be tested. In some cases the specific TASK is identified, in other cases a minimum number of TASKs are identified.

SEE SECTION 2 OF THE PTS

I.   PREFLIGHT PREPARATION

Note: The examiner must select TASKs F and K.

- ☐   A.   Certificates and Documents (PPCL and PPCS)
- ☐   B.   Airworthiness Requirements (PPCL and PPCS)
- ☐   C.   Weather Information (PPCL and PPCS)
- ☐   D.   Cross-Country Flight Planning (PPCL and PPCS)
- ☐   E.   National Airspace System (PPCL and PPCS)
- ☐   **F.   Operation of Systems (PPCL and PPCS)**
- ☐   G.   Aeromedical Factors (PPCL and PPCS)
- ☐   H.   Water and Seaplane Characteristics (PPCS)
- ☐   I.   Seaplane Bases, Maritime Rules, and Aids to Marine Navigation (PPCS)
- ☐   J.   Performance and Limitations (PPCL and PPCS)
- ☐   **K.   Principles of Flight (PPCL and PPCS)**

II.   PREFLIGHT PROCEDURES

Note: The instructor must select TASKs B and E.

- ☐   A.   Preflight Inspection (PPCL and PPCS)
- ☐   **B.   Canopy Layout (PPCL and PPCS)**
- ☐   C.   Engine Warm Up/Starting (PPCL and PPCS)
- ☐   D.   Cockpit Management (PPCL and PPCS)
- ☐   **E.   Taxiing (Canopy Inflated) (PPCL and PPCS)**
- ☐   F.   Taxiing and Sailing (PPCS)
- ☐   G.   Before Takeoff Check (PPCL and PPCS)

III.   AIRPORT AND SEAPLANE BASE OPERATIONS

Note: The instructor must select TASK C.

- ☐   A.   Radio Communications (PPCL and PPCS)
- ☐   B.   Traffic Patterns (PPCL and PPCS)
- ☐   **C.   Airport Runway Markings and Lighting (PPCL and PPCS)**

IV. TAKEOFFS, LANDINGS, AND GO-AROUNDS

Note: The instructor must select TASK G and one takeoff/landing TASK.

☐ A. Normal Takeoff and Climb (PPCL and PPCS)
☐ B. Normal Approach and Landing (PPCL and PPCS)
☐ C. Glassy Water Takeoff and Climb (PPCS)
☐ D. Glassy Water Approach and Landing (PPCS)
☐ E. Rough Water Takeoff and Climb (PPCS)
☐ F. Rough Water Approach and Landing (PPCS)
☐ **G. Go-around/Rejected Landing (PPCL and PPCS)**

V. PERFORMANCE MANEUVER

Note: The instructor must select TASK A.

☐ **A. Constant Attitude Turns (PPCL and PPCS)**

VI. GROUND REFERENCE MANEUVERS

Note: The instructor must select one TASK.

☐ A. Rectangular Course (PPCL and PPCS)
☐ B. S-Turns (PPCL and PPCS)
☐ C. Turns Around a Point (PPCL and PPCS)

VII. NAVIGATION

Note: The instructor must select one TASK.

☐ A. Pilotage (PPCL and PPCS)
☐ B. Diversion (PPCL and PPCS)
☐ A. Lost Procedures (PPCL and PPCS)

VIII. EMERGENCY OPERATIONS

Note: The instructor must select TASK A.

☐ **A. Emergency Approach and Landing (Simulated) (PPCL and PPCS)**
☐ B. Systems and Equipment Malfunctions (PPCL and PPCS)
☐ C. Emergency Equipment and Survival Gear (PPCL and PPCS)

IX. POSTFLIGHT PROCEDURES

Note: The instructor must select TASK A and one other TASK for PPCS.

- ☐ **A. After Landing, Parking, and Securing (PPCL and PPCS)**
- ☐ B. Anchoring (PPCS)
- ☐ C. Docking and Mooring (PPCS)
- ☐ D. Ramping/Beaching (PPCS)

FLIGHT INSTRUCTOR CERTIFICATE WITH SPORT PILOT PRIVILEGES

Flight Instructor Practical Test Section Description

This section provides guidance and procedures for obtaining a Flight Instructor Certificate with a sport pilot rating and for adding privileges to an existing Flight Instructor Certificate at the sport pilot level. Information provided in the Introduction of this practical test standard also applies to this section.

The examiner or authorized instructor determines that the applicant meets the TASK Objective through the demonstration of competency in all elements of knowledge and/or skill unless otherwise noted. The Objectives of TASKs in certain AREAS OF OPERATION, such as Fundamentals of Instructing and Technical Subjects, include only knowledge elements. Objectives of TASKs in AREAS OF OPERATION that include elements of skill, as well as knowledge, also include common errors, which the applicant shall be able to describe, recognize, analyze, and correct.

The word "examiner" is used throughout the standards to denote either the FAA inspector or an FAA designated pilot examiner who conducts an official practical test or proficiency check. When an examiner conducts a proficiency check they are acting in the capacity of an authorized instructor.

At the flight instructor level, the Objective of a TASK that involves pilot skill consists of four parts. The four parts include determination that the applicant exhibits:

1. instructional knowledge of the elements of a TASK. This is accomplished through descriptions, explanations, and simulated instruction;
2. instructional knowledge of common errors related to a TASK, including their recognition, analysis, and correction;
3. able to perform the procedures and maneuvers included in the standards at a more precise level than that indicated in the sport pilot tolerances; and
4. the ability to analyze and correct common errors related to a TASK.

Use of the Flight Instructor Section

The FAA requires that all flight instructor practical tests and proficiency checks be conducted in accordance with the policies set forth in this practical test standard. The flight instructor applicant must be prepared to demonstrate the ability to instruct effectively in **ALL** TASKs included in the AREAS OF OPERATION appropriate to the category/class unless otherwise noted.

A proficiency check is an evaluation of aeronautical knowledge and flight proficiency IAW 14 CFR part 61.419. A proficiency check shall be administered using the appropriate PTS for the category of aircraft when a pilot or a flight instructor adds new category/class privileges. Upon successful completion of the proficiency check the authorized instructor will endorse the applicant's logbook indicating the added category/class of equipment that the applicant is authorized to operate. When an examiner conducts a proficiency check they are acting in the capacity of an authorized instructor.

All of the procedures and maneuvers to be tested are included in the sport pilot practical test standards. The flight instructor section contains the AREAS OF OPERATION that are generic to all flight instructor evaluations. Flight instructors must also be tested on TASKS located in the appropriate category/class section the PTS. Those TASKs are listed in the examiner's practical test checklist and the instructor's proficiency check checklist. The mandatory TASKs are identified by a note located in each area of operation. In some cases specific TASKs are identified. In other cases the examiner/instructor selects one or more TASKs in an area of operation for evaluation. This allows for the practical test for initial certification and additional privileges to be completed within a reasonable time frame.

The term "instructional knowledge" means the instructor applicant is capable of using the appropriate reference to provide the "application or correlative level of knowledge" of a subject matter topic, procedure, or maneuver. It also means that the flight instructor applicant's discussions, explanations, and descriptions should follow the recommended teaching procedures and techniques explained in FAA-H-8083-9, Aviation Instructor's Handbook.

In preparation for the practical test or proficiency check, the examiner or authorized instructor shall develop a written "plan of action." The "plan of action" for an initial certification test shall include the required Tasks and one or more TASKs in the *Fundamentals of Instruction*, *Technical Subject Area* and the *Preflight Lesson on a Maneuver to be Preformed in Flight* AREAS OF OPERATION. Additionally, the examiner shall test the required TASK(s) listed in the examiner's practical test checklist, for the appropriate category. The "plan of action" must **always** include the required TASKs noted in each AREA OF OPERATION. **Any TASK selected shall be evaluated in its entirety.**

If the applicant is unable to perform a TASK listed in the "plan of action" due to circumstances beyond his/her control, the examiner or authorized instructor may substitute another TASK from the applicable AREA OF OPERATION.

The "plan of action" used by an authorized instructor for a proficiency check administered for the addition of an aircraft category and/or class privilege to a Flight Instructor Certificate shall include TASKs required in the AREAS OF OPERATION as indicated in the instructor's proficiency check checklist located in this section.

With the exception of the required TASKs, the examiner or authorized instructor shall not tell the applicant in advance which TASKs will be included in the "plan of action." The applicant shall be prepared in **ALL** knowledge and skill areas included in the standards. Throughout the flight portion of the practical test or proficiency check, the examiner or authorized instructor shall evaluate the applicant's ability to simultaneously demonstrate and explain procedures and maneuvers, and to give flight instruction to students at various stages of flight training and levels of experience.

The examiner or authorized instructor is expected to use good judgment in the performance of simulated emergency procedures. The examiner or authorized instructor shall not simulate any condition that may jeopardize safe flight or result in possible damage to the aircraft. The use of the safest means for simulation is expected. Consideration must be given to local conditions, both meteorological and topographical, at the time of the test, as well as the applicant's workload, and the condition of the aircraft used. If the procedure being evaluated would jeopardize safety, it is expected that the applicant will simulate that portion of the maneuver.

Special Emphasis Areas

Examiners or authorized instructors shall place special emphasis upon areas of aircraft operations considered critical to flight safety. Among these are:

1. positive aircraft control;
2. procedures for positive exchange of flight controls (who is flying the aircraft);
3. stall and spin awareness (if appropriate);
4. collision avoidance;
5. wake turbulence and low level windshear avoidance;
6. runway incursion avoidance;
7. controlled flight into terrain (CFIT);
8. aeronautical decision making /risk management;
9. checklist usage;
10. temporary flight restrictions (TFR);

11. special use airspace (SUA);
12. aviation security;
13. spatial disorientation; and
14. other areas deemed appropriate to any phase of the practical test or proficiency check.

The examiner or authorized instructor shall place special emphasis on the applicant's demonstrated ability to teach precise aircraft control and sound judgment in aeronautical decision making/risk management. Evaluation of the applicant's ability to teach judgment shall be accomplished by asking the applicant to describe the presentation of practical problems that would be used in instructing students in the exercise of sound judgment. The examiner or authorized instructor shall also emphasize the evaluation of the applicant's demonstrated ability to teach the special emphasis areas.

Although these areas may not be specifically addressed under each TASK, they are essential to flight safety and will be evaluated during the practical test. In all instances, the applicant's actions will be evaluated in accordance to the standards of the tasks and the ability to use good judgment reference the special emphasis areas listed above.

Sport Pilot Flight Instructor Prerequisites—Initial

An applicant for a flight instructor—initial certification practical test is to:

1. be at least 18 years of age;
2. be able to read, speak, write, and understand the English language. If there is a doubt, use AC 60-28, English Language Skill Standards required by 14 CFR part 61;
3. hold at least a current and valid Sport Pilot Certificate or higher with an aircraft category and class, privilege or rating appropriate to the flight instructor rating sought;
4. have passed the fundamentals of instructing knowledge test since the beginning of the 24th month before the month in which he/she takes the practical test or meet the requirements of 14 CFR part 61;
5. have passed the appropriate sport pilot flight instructor knowledge test(s) appropriate to the category/class the applicant is since the beginning of the 24th month before the month in which he/she takes the practical test; and

6. have an endorsement from an authorized instructor certifying that the applicant has been given flight training in the AREAS OF OPERATION specified in 14 CFR part 61 and a written statement from an authorized flight instructor within the preceding 60 days, in accordance with section 61.39, that instruction was given in preparation for the practical test. The endorsement shall also state that the instructor finds the applicant prepared for the required practical test, and that the applicant has demonstrated satisfactory knowledge of the subject area(s) in which the applicant was deficient on the airman knowledge test.

Sport Pilot Flight Instructor Prerequisites—Additional Privileges

A certificated flight instructor seeking privileges to provide flight training in an additional category/class of light-sport aircraft is required by 14 CFR part 61 to:

1. hold a valid pilot certificate with ratings appropriate to the flight instructor category and class, privileges or rating sought;
2. receive a logbook endorsement from an authorized instructor in the AREAS OF OPERATION specified in 14 CFR part 61 for the additional category/class privilege sought;
3. successfully pass a proficiency check from an authorized instructor other than the instructor who conducted the training in the AREAS OF OPERATION specified in 14 CFR part 61 for the additional category/class privilege sought; and
4. receive a logbook endorsement certifying proficiency in the required AREAS OF OPERATION and authorized for the additional category/class privilege.

Sport Pilot Flight Instructor Prerequisites—Additional Privileges—Registered Ultra-light Instructor

If you are a registered ultra-light instructor with an FAA-recognized ultra-light organization on or before September 1, 2004, and you want to apply for a flight instructor certificate with a sport pilot rating, not later than January 31, 2008—

1. You must hold either a current and valid Sport Pilot Certificate, a current Recreational Pilot Certificate and meet the requirements of 14 CFR part 61, section 61.101(c), or at least a current and valid Private Pilot Certificate issued under this part.
2. You must meet the eligibility requirements in 14 CFR part 61, sections 61.403 and 61.23. You do not have to meet the aeronautical knowledge requirements specified in section 61.407, the flight proficiency requirements specified in section 61.409 and the aeronautical experience requirements specified in section 61.411, except you must meet the minimum total flight time requirements in the category and class of light-sport aircraft specified in section 61.411.
3. You do not have to meet the aeronautical knowledge requirement specified in 14 CFR part 61, section 61.407(a) if you have passed an FAA-recognized ultra-light organization's fundamentals of instruction knowledge test.
4. You must submit a certified copy of your ultra light pilot records from the FAA-recognized ultra-light organization. Those records must—

    a. Document that you are a registered ultra-light flight instructor with that FAA-recognized ultra-light organization; and
    b. Indicate that you are recognized to operate and provide training in the category and class of aircraft for which you seek privileges.

5. You must pass the knowledge test and practical test for a flight instructor certificate with a sport pilot rating applicable to the aircraft category and class for which you seek flight instructor privileges.

Flight Instructor Responsibility

An appropriately rated flight instructor is responsible for training the flight instructor applicant to acceptable standards in **ALL** subject matter areas, procedures, and maneuvers included in the TASKs within each AREA OF OPERATION in the appropriate category/class in this practical test standard. In addition, the rated flight instructor is required to prepare the flight instructor applicant in all tasks in the AREAS OF OPERATION listed in Section 3.

Because of the impact of their teaching activities in developing safe, proficient pilots, flight instructors should exhibit a high level of knowledge, skill, and the ability to impart that knowledge and skill to students. The flight instructor must certify that the applicant is:

1. able to make a practical application of the fundamentals of instructing;
2. competent to teach the subject matter, procedures, and maneuvers included in the standards to students with varying backgrounds and levels of experience and ability;
3. able to perform the procedures and maneuvers included in the standards at a more precise level than that required at the sport pilot level; and
4. competent to pass the required practical test for the issuance of the Flight Instructor Certificate—Sport Pilot with the associated category/class privileges or the addition of a category/class privileges.

Throughout the flight instructor applicant's training, the flight instructor is responsible for emphasizing the performance of, and the ability to teach, effective visual scanning, runway incursion avoidance, and collision avoidance procedures. The flight instructor applicant should develop and use scenario based teaching methods particularly on special emphasis areas. These areas are covered in AC 90-48, Pilot's Role in Collision Avoidance; FAA-H-8083-3, Airplane Flying Handbook; FAA-H-8083-11, Balloon Flying Handbook; FAA-H-8083-13, Glider Flying Handbook; FAA-H-8083-21, Rotorcraft Flying Handbook; FAA-H-8083-23, Seaplane, Skiplane and Float/Ski Equipped Helicopter Handbook; FAA-H-8083-25, Pilot's Handbook of Aeronautical Knowledge; and the *current* Aeronautical Information Manual.

Examiner Responsibility

The examiner conducting the practical test or the authorized instructor conducting the proficiency check is responsible for determining that the applicant meets acceptable standards of teaching ability, knowledge, and skill in the selected TASKs. The examiner or authorized instructor makes this determination by accomplishing an Objective that is appropriate to each selected TASK, and includes an evaluation of the applicant's:

1. ability to apply the fundamentals of instructing;
2. knowledge of, and ability to teach, the subject matter, procedures, and maneuvers covered in the TASKs;
3. able to perform the procedures and maneuvers included in the standards at a more precise level than that indicated in the sport pilot tolerances; and
4. ability to describe, recognize, analyze, and correct common errors related to the skill procedures and maneuvers covered in the TASKs.

It is intended that oral questioning be used at any time during the ground or flight portion of the practical test or proficiency check to determine that the applicant can instruct effectively and has a comprehensive knowledge of the TASKs and their related safety factors.

During the flight portion of the practical test the examiner or during proficiency check the authorized instructor shall act as a student during selected maneuvers. This will give the examiner or authorized instructor an opportunity to evaluate the flight instructor applicant's ability to analyze and correct simulated common errors related to these maneuvers. The examiner or authorized instructor will place special emphasis on the applicant's use of visual scanning and collision avoidance procedures, and the applicant's ability to teach those procedures.

Examiners or authorized instructors should to the greatest extent possible test the applicant's application and correlation skills. When possible scenario based questions should be used during the practical test or proficiency check.

If the examiner or authorized instructor determines that a TASK is incomplete, or the outcome uncertain, the examiner or authorized instructor may require the applicant to repeat that TASK, or portions of that TASK. This provision has been made in the interest of fairness and does not mean that instruction, practice or the repeating of an unsatisfactory task is permitted during the certification process. When practical, the remaining TASKs of the practical test or proficiency check phase should be completed before repeating the questionable TASK.

Initial Flight Instructor Certification Check—Satisfactory Performance

An applicant who seeks initial flight instructor certification will be evaluated in all AREAS OF OPERATION of the standards appropriate to the category/class privileges sought. The examiner shall refer to the examiner's practical test checklist, for the appropriate category, located in this section, to determine the TASKs to be tested, in each AREA OF OPERATION.

The practical test is passed if, in the judgment of the examiner, the applicant demonstrates satisfactory performance with regard to:

1. knowledge of the fundamentals of instructing;
2. knowledge of the technical subject areas;
3. knowledge of the flight instructor's responsibilities concerning the pilot certification process;

4. knowledge of the flight instructor's responsibilities concerning logbook entries and pilot certificate endorsements;
5. able to perform the procedures and maneuvers included in the standards at a more precise level than that indicated in the sport pilot tolerances while giving effective instruction;
6. competence in teaching the procedures and maneuvers selected by the examiner;
7. competence in describing, recognizing, analyzing, and correcting common errors simulated by the examiner; and
8. knowledge of the development and effective use of a course of training, a syllabus, and a lesson plan.

Initial Flight Instructor Certification Check—Unsatisfactory Performance

If, in the judgment of the examiner, the applicant does not meet the standards of performance of any TASK performed, the applicable AREA OF OPERATION is considered unsatisfactory and therefore, the practical test or proficiency check is failed. The examiner or applicant may discontinue the test at any time when the failure of an AREA OF OPERATION makes the applicant ineligible for the certificate or rating sought. **The test will be continued only with the consent of the applicant.**

If the test is discontinued, the applicant is entitled credit for only those AREAS OF OPERATION and their associated TASKs satisfactorily performed. However, during the retest and at the discretion of the examiner, any TASK may be re-evaluated, including those previously considered satisfactory.

A specific reason for disqualification is:

1. failure to perform a procedure or maneuver at a more precise level than that indicated in the Sport Pilot tolerances while giving effective flight instruction;
2. failure to provide an effective instructional explanation while demonstrating a procedure or maneuver (explanation during the demonstration must be clear, concise, technically accurate, and complete with no prompting from the examiner);
3. any action or lack of action by the applicant which requires corrective intervention by the examiner to maintain safe flight; or
4. failure to use proper and effective visual scanning techniques to clear the area before and while performing maneuvers.

Change 1 (6/9/06)

When a Disapproval Notice is issued, the examiner shall record the applicant's unsatisfactory performance in terms of AREA(s) OF OPERATIONS and specific TASK(s) not meeting the standard appropriate to the practical test conducted. If the applicant fails the practical test because of a special emphasis area, the Notice of Disapproval shall indicate the associated TASK. AN EXAMPLE WOULD BE: AREA OF OPERATION VI, TRAFFIC PATTERNS, FAILURE TO TEACH PROPER COLLISION AVOIDANCE PROCEDURES.

Proficiency Check—Satisfactory Performance When Adding Additional Category/Class Privileges

The authorized instructor shall refer to the instructor's proficiency check checklist, for the appropriate category, located in this section, to determine the TASKs to be tested, in each AREA OF OPERATION. The proficiency check is passed if, in the judgment of the authorized instructor, the applicant demonstrates satisfactory performance with regard to:

1. knowledge of the fundamentals of instructing;
2. knowledge of the technical subject areas;
3. knowledge of the flight instructor's responsibilities concerning the pilot certification process;
4. knowledge of the flight instructor's responsibilities concerning logbook entries and pilot certificate endorsements;
5. be able to perform the procedures and maneuvers included in the standards at a more precise level than that indicated in the Sport Pilot tolerances while giving effective instruction;
6. competence in teaching the procedures and maneuvers selected by the examiner;
7. competence in describing, recognizing, analyzing, and correcting common errors simulated by the examiner; and
8. knowledge of the development and effective use of a course of training, a syllabus, and a lesson plan.

When an applicant is adding a category/class privileges to their Flight Instructor Certificate, the evaluating authorized instructor shall, upon successful completion of the proficiency check, endorse the applicant's logbook indicating that the applicant is qualified to instruct in an additional sport pilot category/class of aircraft. The authorized instructor shall forward FAA Form 8710-11 to Airman Registry within 10 days.

Proficiency Check—Unsatisfactory Performance When Adding Additional Category/Class Privileges

When the applicant's performance does not meet the standards in the PTS, the authorized instructor conducting the proficiency check shall annotate the unsatisfactory performance on the FAA Form 8710-11 and forward it to Airman Registry within 10 days. A Notice of Disapproval will **NOT** be issued in this instance; rather, the applicant should be provided with a list of the AREAS OF OPERATION and the specific TASKs not meeting the standard, so that the applicant may receive additional training.

A specific reason for disqualification is:

1.   failure to perform a procedure or maneuver at a more precise level than that indicated in the Sport Pilot tolerances while giving effective flight instruction;

2.   failure to provide an effective instructional explanation while demonstrating a procedure or maneuver (explanation during the demonstration must be clear, concise, technically accurate, and complete with no prompting from the authorized instructor);

3.   any action or lack of action by the applicant which requires corrective intervention by the examiner to maintain safe flight; or

4.   failure to use proper and effective visual scanning techniques to clear the area before and while performing maneuvers.

When the applicant receives the additional training in the AREAS OF OPERATION and the specific TASK(s) found deficient during the proficiency check, the recommending instructor shall endorse the applicant's logbook indicating that the applicant has received additional instruction and has been found competent to pass the proficiency check. The applicant shall complete a new FAA Form 8710-11, and the recommending instructor shall endorse the application. The authorized instructor, other than the one who provided the additional training, shall evaluate the applicant. When the applicant successfully accomplishes a complete proficiency check, the authorized instructor, shall forward the FAA Form 8710-11 to Airman Registry within 10 days and indorse the applicant's logbook indicating the airman's additional privileges.

Renewal or Reinstatement of a Flight Instructor Certificate

14 CFR part 61, sections 61.197(a)(1) and 61.199(a) allow an individual that holds a Flight Instructor Certificate to renew or reinstate that certificate by passing a practical test. The examiner shall develop a plan of action that includes at least one TASK, in each AREA OF OPERATION, in the examiner's practical test checklist, located in this section, for the appropriate category. The Renewal or Reinstatement of one rating on a Flight Instructor Certificate renews or reinstates all privileges existing on the certificate.

I. AREA OF OPERATION: FUNDAMENTALS OF INSTRUCTING

NOTE: The examiner shall select TASK F and one other TASK.

A. TASK: THE LEARNING PROCESS

REFERENCE: FAA-H-8083-9.

Objective.   To determine that the applicant exhibits instructional knowledge of the elements of the learning process by describing:

  1.   Learning theory.
  2.   Characteristics of learning.
  3.   Principles of learning.
  4.   Levels of learning.
  5.   Learning physical skills.
  6.   Memory.
  7.   Transfer of learning.

B.   TASK: HUMAN BEHAVIOR AND EFFECTIVE COMMUNICATION

REFERENCE: FAA-H-8083-9.

Objective.   To determine that the applicant exhibits instructional knowledge of the elements of the teaching process by describing:

  1.   Human behavior—

      a.   control of human behavior.
      b.   human needs.
      c.   defense mechanisms.
      d.   the flight instructor as a practical psychologist.

  2.   Effective communication—

      a.   basic elements of communication.
      b.   barriers of effective communication.
      c.   developing communication skills.

C. TASK: THE TEACHING PROCESS

REFERENCE: FAA-H-8083-9.

Objective. To determine that the applicant exhibits instructional knowledge of the elements of the teaching process by describing:

1. Preparation of a lesson for a ground or flight instructional period.
2. Presentation methods.
3. Application, by the student, of the material or procedure presented.
4. Review and evaluation of student performance.

D. TASK: TEACHING METHODS

REFERENCE: FAA-H-8083-9.

Objective. To determine that the applicant exhibits instructional knowledge of the elements of teaching methods by describing:

1. Material organization.
2. The lecture method.
3. The cooperative or group learning method.
4. The guided discussion method.
5. The demonstration-performance method.
6. Computer-based training method.

E. TASK: CRITIQUE AND EVALUATION

REFERENCE: FAA-H-8083-9.

Objective. To determine that the applicant exhibits instructional knowledge of the elements of critique and evaluation by explaining:

1. Critique—

   a. purpose and characteristics of an effective critique.
   b. methods and ground rules for a critique.

2. Evaluation—

   a. characteristics of effective oral questions and what types to avoid.
   b. responses to student questions.
   c. characteristics and development of effective written questions.
   d. characteristics and uses of performance test, specifically, the FAA practical test standards.

F. TASK: FLIGHT INSTRUCTOR CHARACTERISTICS AND RESPONSIBILITIES

REFERENCE: FAA-H-8083-9.

Objective.   To determine that the applicant exhibits instructional knowledge of the elements of flight instructor characteristics and responsibilities by describing:

1.   Aviation instructor responsibilities in—

   a.   providing adequate instruction.
   b.   establishing standards of performance.
   c.   emphasizing the positive.
   d.   developing plans of action for use during proficiency checks.
   e.   completion of FAA Form 8710-11.

2.   Flight instructor responsibilities in—

   a.   providing student pilot evaluation and supervision.
   b.   preparing practical test recommendations and endorsements.
   c.   determining requirements for conducting additional training and endorsement requirements.
   d.   conducting proficiency checks for additional category/class privileges.

3.   Professionalism as an instructor by—

   a.   explaining important personal characteristics.
   b.   describing methods to minimize student frustration.

G. TASK: PLANNING INSTRUCTIONAL ACTIVITY

REFERENCE: FAA-H-8083-9.

Objective.   To determine that the applicant exhibits instructional knowledge of the elements of planning instructional activity by describing:

1.   Developing objectives and standards for a course of training.
2.   Theory of building blocks of learning.
3.   Requirements for developing a training syllabus.
4.   Purpose and characteristics of a lesson plan.

II. AREA OF OPERATION: TECHNICAL SUBJECT AREAS

NOTE: The examiner shall select TASK D and at least one other TASK.

A. TASK: AEROMEDICAL FACTORS

REFERENCES: FAA-H-8083-3; FAA-S-8081-12, FAA-S-8081-14; AIM.

Objective. To determine that the applicant exhibits instructional knowledge of the elements related to aeromedical factors by describing:

1. How to obtain an appropriate medical certificate.
2. How to obtain a medical certificate in the event of a possible medical deficiency.
3. The causes, symptoms, effects, and corrective action of the following medical factors—

   a. hypoxia.
   b. hyperventilation.
   c. middle ear and sinus problems.
   d. spatial disorientation.
   e. motion sickness.
   f. carbon monoxide poisoning.
   g. fatigue and stress.
   h. dehydration.
   i. hypothermia.

4. The effects of alcohol and drugs, and their relationship to flight safety.

B. TASK: VISUAL SCANNING AND COLLISION AVOIDANCE

REFERENCES: FAA-H-8083-3, FAA-H-8083-25; AC 90-48; AIM.

Objective. To determine that the applicant exhibits instructional knowledge of the elements of visual scanning and collision avoidance by describing:

1. Relationship between a pilot's physical condition and vision.
2. Environmental conditions that degrade vision.
3. Vestibular and visual illusions.
4. "See and avoid" concept.
5. Proper visual scanning procedure.
6. Relationship between poor visual scanning habits and increased collision risk.
7. Proper clearing procedures.
8. Importance of knowing aircraft blind spots.
9. Relationship between aircraft speed differential and collision risk.
10. Situations that involve the greatest collision risk.

C. TASK: FEDERAL AVIATION REGULATIONS AND PUBLICATIONS

REFERENCES: 14 CFR parts 1, 61, 91; NTSB part 830; AC 00-2,
FAA-H-8083-25; Aircraft Flight Manual/POH; AIM.

Objective. To determine that the applicant exhibits instructional knowledge of the elements related to Code of Federal Regulations and publications:

1. Availability and method of revision of 14 CFR parts 1, 61, 91, and NTSB part 830 by describing—

   a. purpose.
   b. general content.

2. Availability of flight information publications, advisory circulars, practical test standards, pilot operating handbooks, and FAA-approved flight manuals by describing—

   a. availability.
   b. purpose.
   c. general content.

D. TASK: LOGBOOK ENTRIES AND CERTIFICATE ENDORSEMENTS

REFERENCES: 14 CFR part 61; AC 61-65.

Objective. To determine that the applicant exhibits instructional knowledge of the elements related to logbook entries and certificate endorsements by describing

1. Required logbook entries for instruction given.
2. Required student pilot certificate endorsements, including appropriate logbook entries.
3. Preparation of a recommendation for a pilot practical test/proficiency check, including appropriate logbook entry for—

   a. initial pilot certification.
   b. additional pilot certification.
   c. additional aircraft category/class privileges.
   d. make and model privileges.
   e. single-seat aircraft.

4. Required endorsement of a pilot logbook for the satisfactory completion of the required FAA flight review.
5. Required flight instructor records.

III. AREA OF OPERATION: PREFLIGHT LESSON ON A MANEUVER TO BE PERFORMED IN FLIGHT

NOTE: Examiner shall select at least one maneuver TASK, and ask the applicant to present a preflight lesson on the selected maneuver as the lesson would be taught to a student.

A. TASK: MANEUVER LESSON

REFERENCES: FAA-H-8083-3, FAA-H-8083-9, FAA-H-8083-25, FAA-H-8083-29; FAA-S-8081-12, FAA-S-8081-14; Aircraft Flight Manual/POH.

Objective. To determine that the applicant exhibits instructional knowledge of the selected maneuver by:

1. Stating the purpose.
2. Giving an accurate, comprehensive oral description, including the elements and common errors.
3. Using instructional aids, as appropriate.
4. Describing the recognition, analysis, and correction of common errors.

Note: Refer to the appropriate checklist for those additional items that must be tested in section 1 or 2 of the PTS.